AMAZING PHOTOS™

MUTT MOMENTS

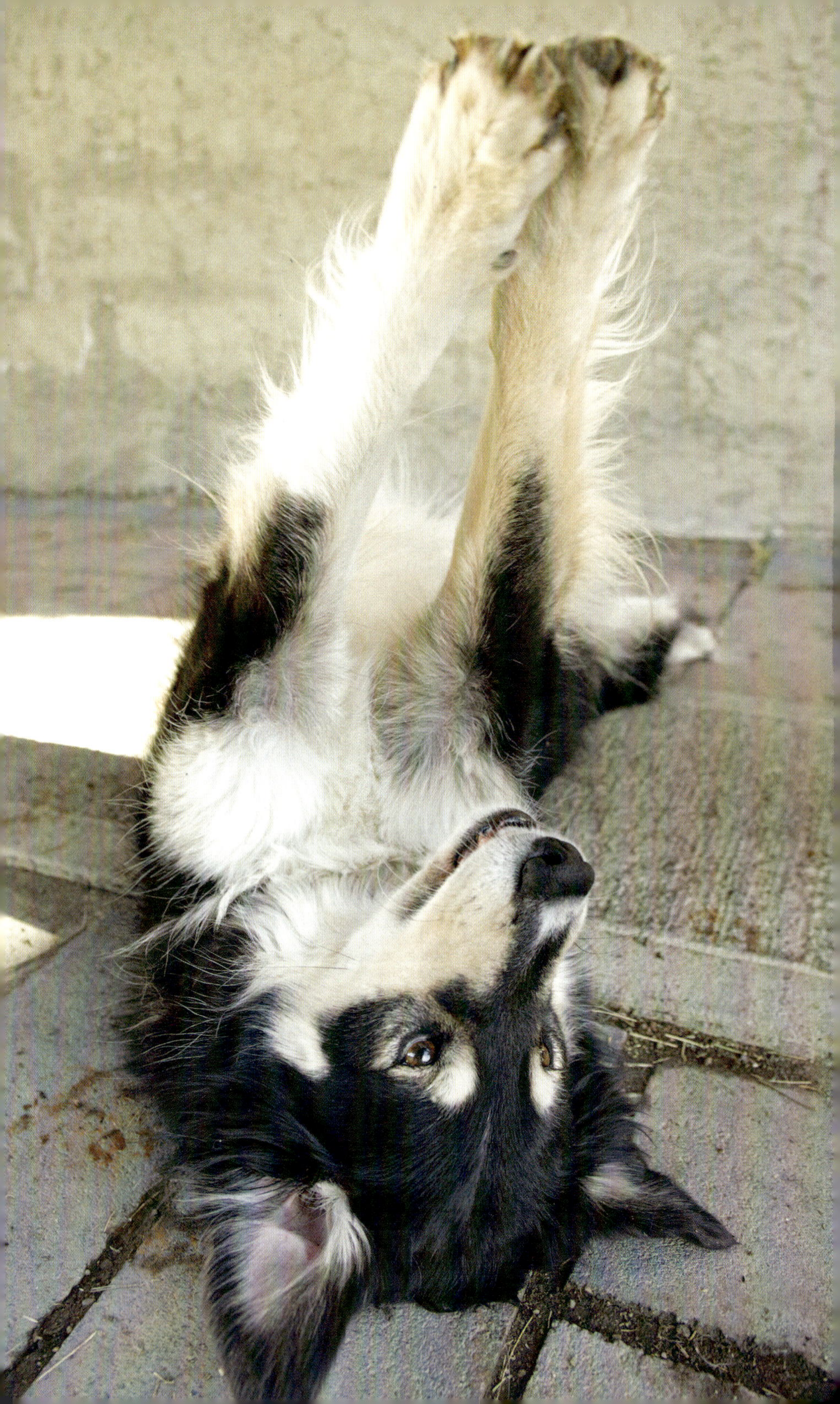

AMAZING PHOTOS™

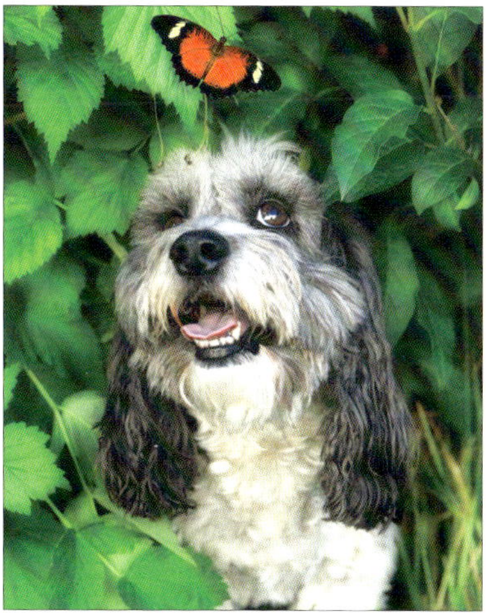

MUTT MOMENTS

Darwin Wiggett

ALTITUDE PUBLISHING

Published by Altitude Publishing Canada Ltd.
1500 Railway Avenue, Canmore, Alberta T1W 1P6
www.altitudepublishing.com
1-800-957-6888

Publisher Stephen Hutchings
Associate Publisher Kara Turner
Design and Photo Editing Stephen Hutchings
Editor Diana Marshall
Layout Bryan Pezzi

We acknowledge the financial support of the Government of Canada through the Book Publishing Industry Development Program (BPIDP) for our publishing activities.

Altitude GreenTree Program: Altitude Publishing will plant twice as many trees as were used in the manufacturing of this product.

Library and Archives Canada Cataloguing in Publication

Wiggett, Darwin, 1961-
Mutt moments / Darwin Wiggett.

(Amazing photos)
ISBN 1-55439-609-3

1. Dogs--Pictorial works. I. Title. II. Series.

SF430.W54 2006 636.70022'2 C2006-903171-1

Printed and bound in Canada by Friesens
2 4 6 8 9 7 5 3 1

INTRODUCTION

Mixed-breed dogs are rarely celebrated. They lack the prestige and pedigree of purebreds. Compared to their purebred counterparts, mutts are downtrodden and rejected; they occupy the second class of the canine world. However, what they lack in athleticism and ancestry, they make up for in their quirky charm, their capacity for love, and their robust nature.

In this book, photographer Darwin Wiggett tips his hat, and his camera lens, to the mutts in our lives. Anyone who has owned and loved one of these canine misfits knows how easily they can wiggle their way into hearts and homes. Mutts often become the "best darned dog" their owners ever had. The photographic vignettes in this collection celebrate the zany, the mischievous, the playful, the quiet, and the tender moments of some beloved mutts.

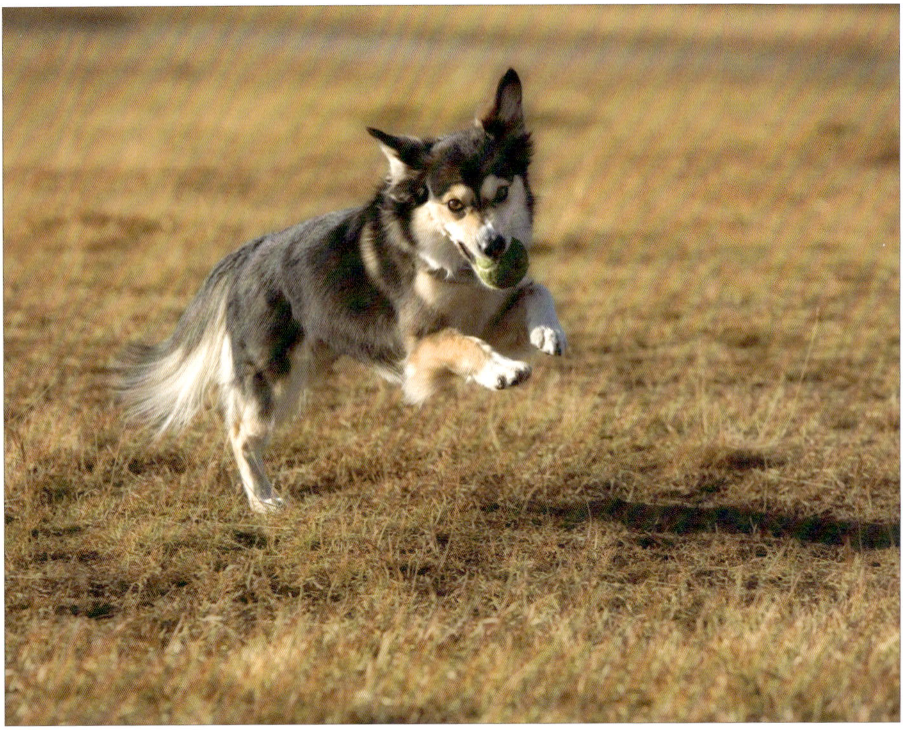

above:
According to her owner, Maddy does not retrieve balls, but to everyone's surprise, Maddy bounded after this ball for half an hour. In fact, she retrieved the ball as if she had been doing so all her life.

opposite:
Shirley (the cat) and Zora (the dog) met for the first time during this photo shoot. As soon as the photo had been snapped, Zora swiped Shirley across the nose. After a brief tussle, in which Shirley bit Zora's leg, the pecking order was established and a friendship began.

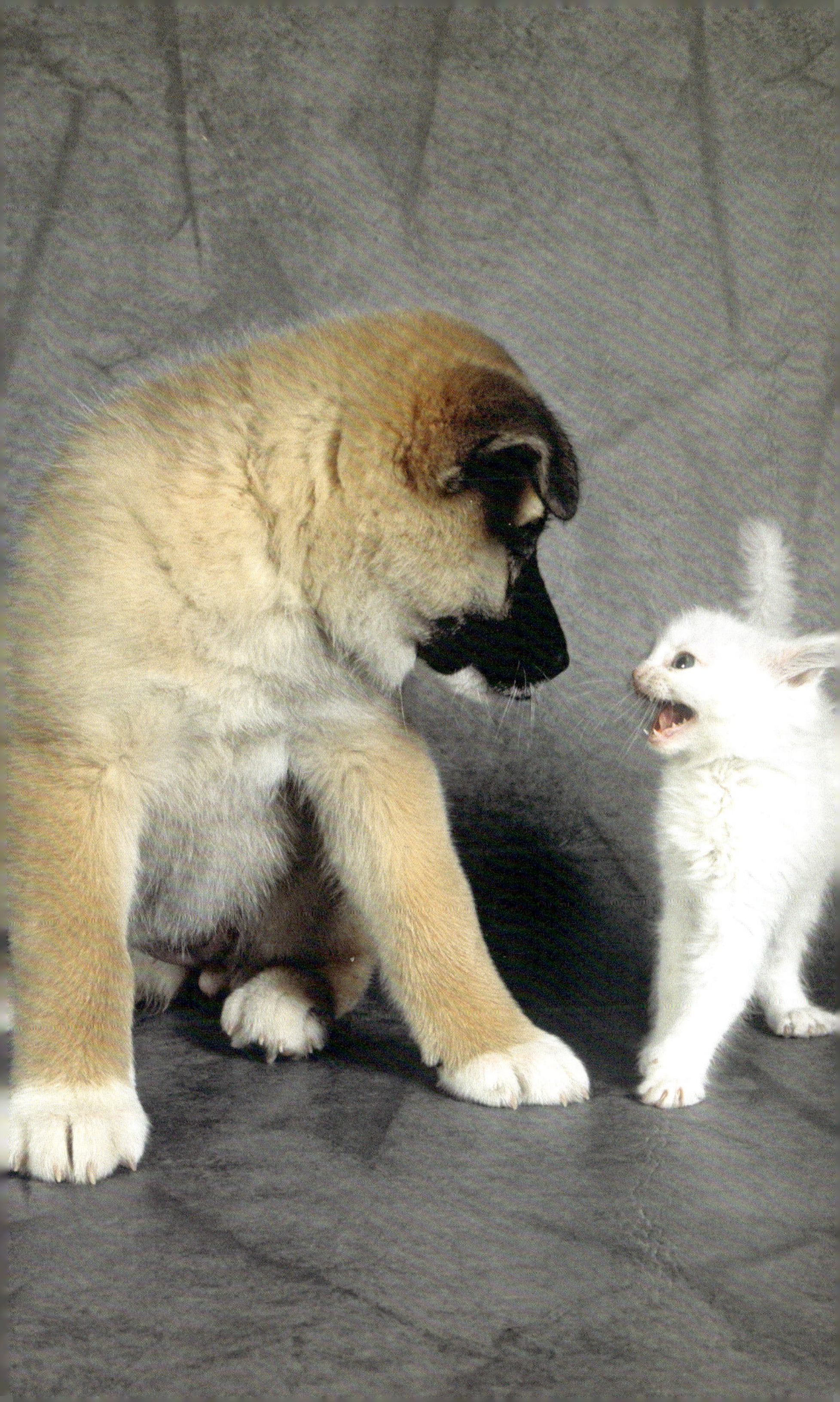

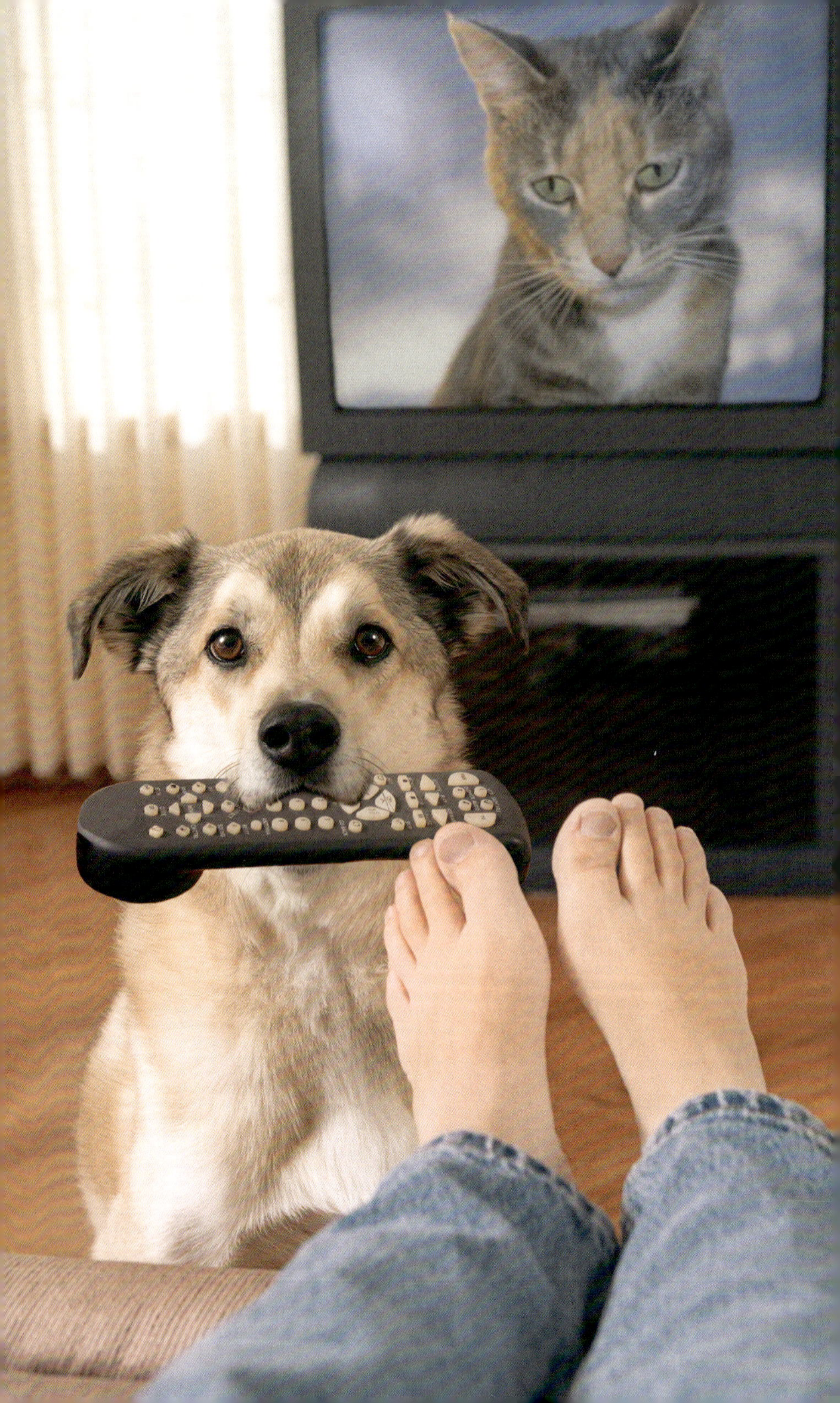

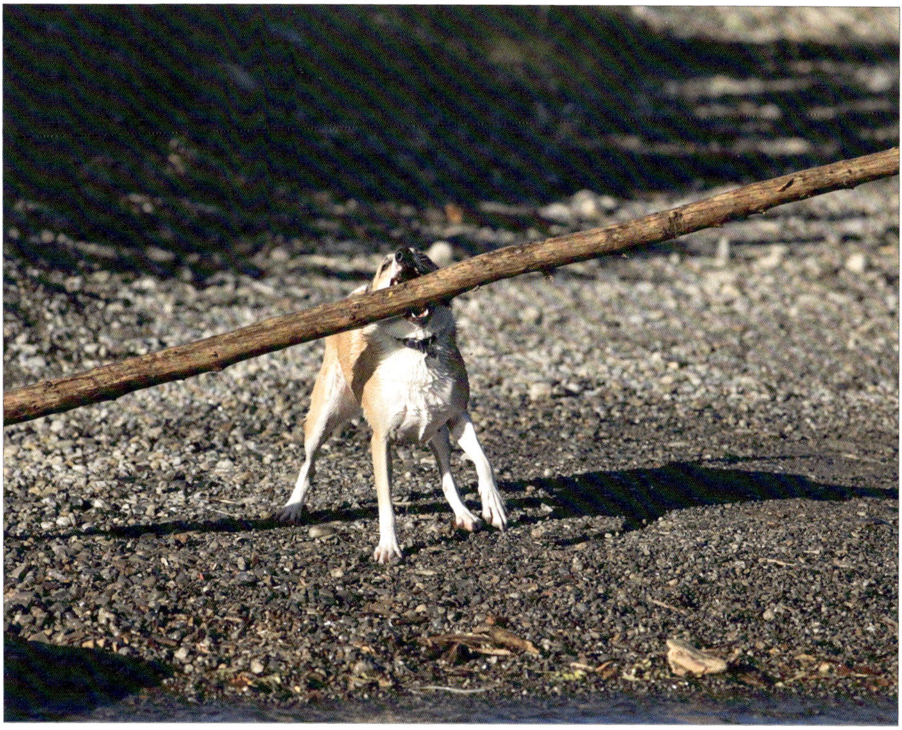

opposite:
Abe enjoys watching television with his owner, but only if he chooses the channel.

above:
Pepper, a Staffordshire bull terrier–collie cross, has the endurance of a collie and the attitude of a Staffy. He loves to take on large logs and tree trunks. In Pepper's world, size definitely does *not* matter.

page 10:
Jigsaw is so named because she is a genetic puzzle. The shelter identified her as a boxer cross. Her owners believe that she is a greyhound crossed with a tree kangaroo, an earthworm, and an alien species!

page 11:
A polite dog, Abby is a Labradoodle — a cross between a Labrador retriever and a standard poodle.

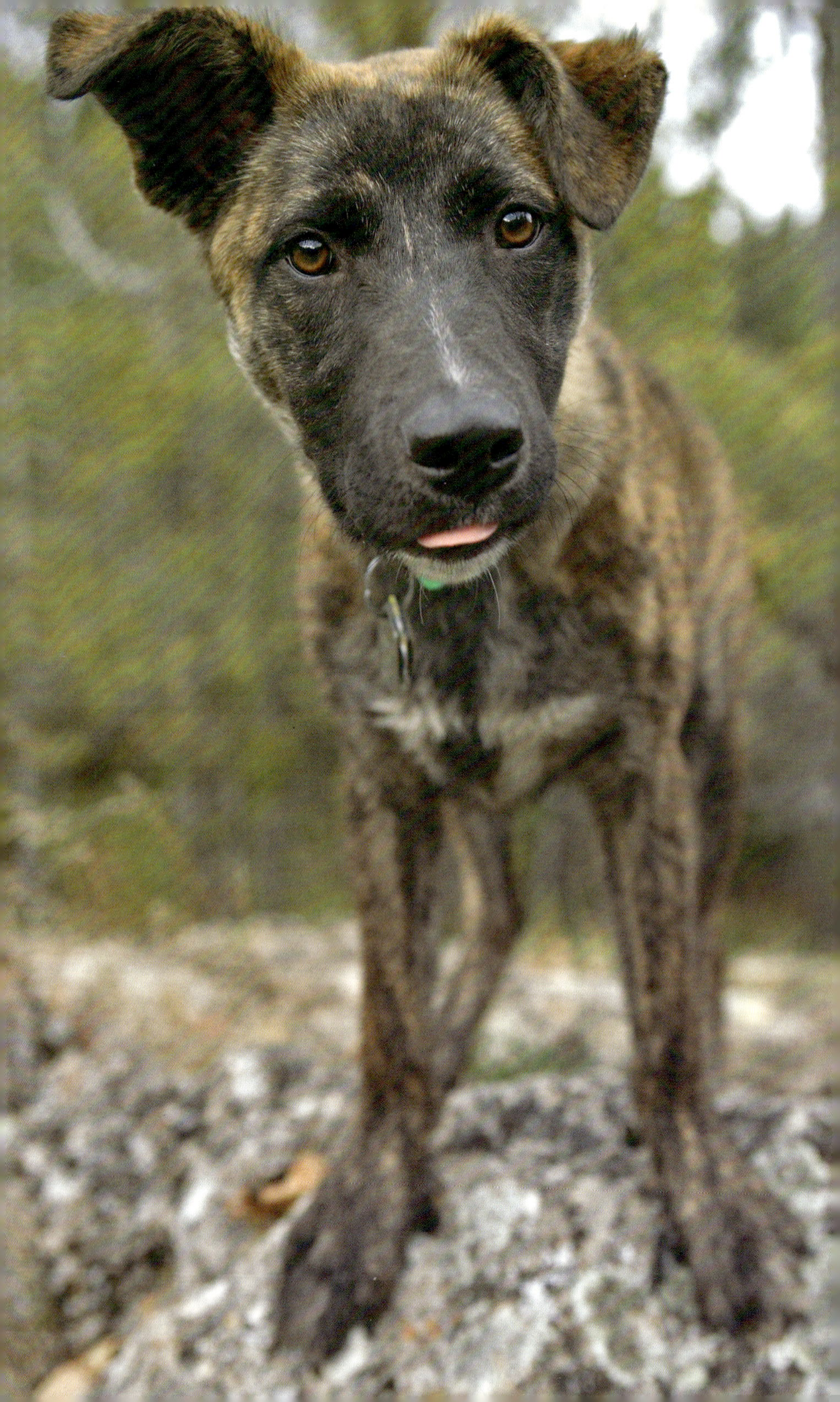

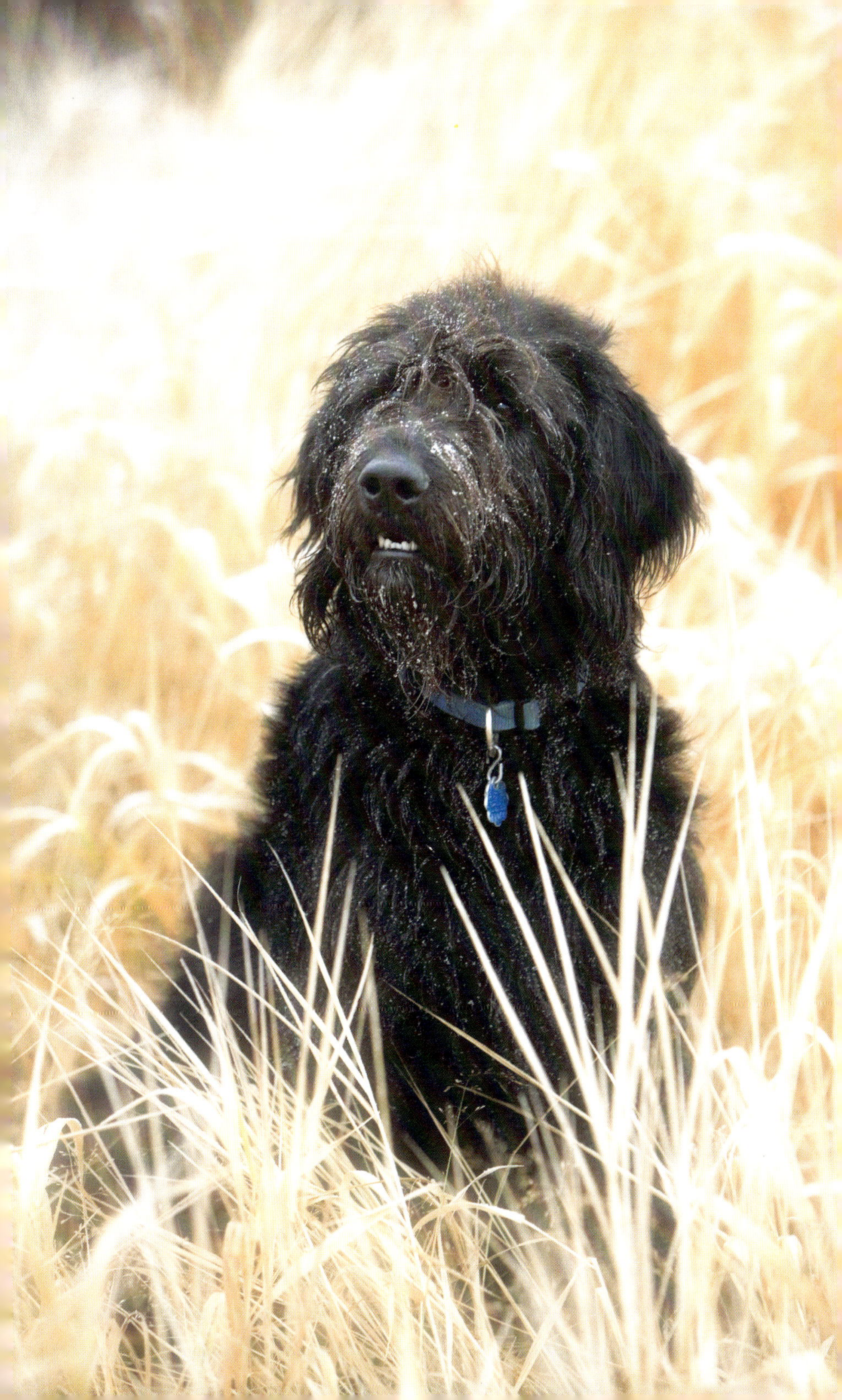

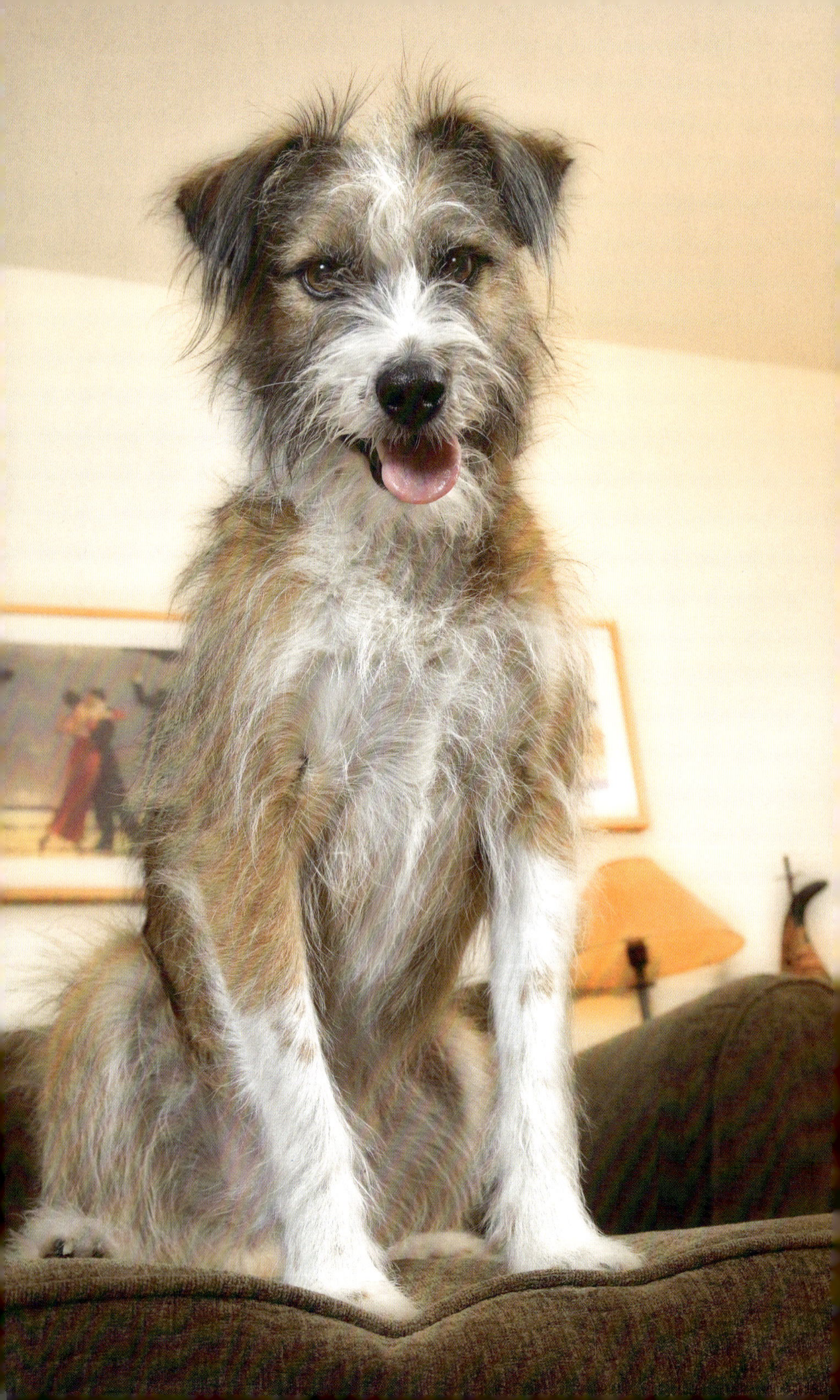

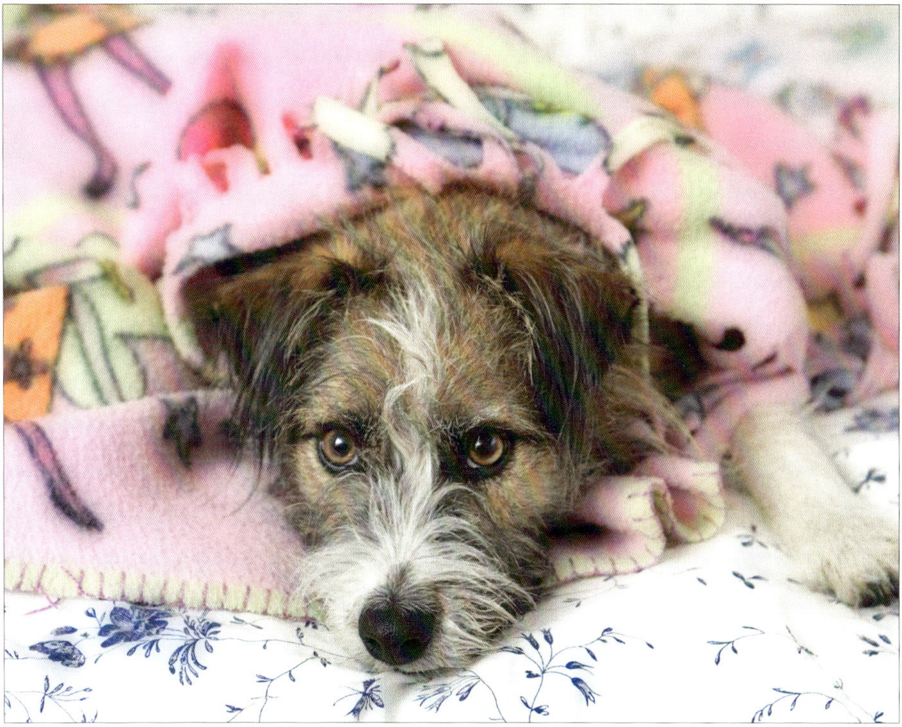

opposite:
Murphy waited patiently at the shelter for his current owners. When they finally arrived, looking for a new dog, he gave them a "what-took-you-so-long-to-get-here" look.

above:
There is a special bond between Murphy and his owners' daughter. Murphy is often found sleeping on her bed, and only she can hold his paw when he gets his shots.

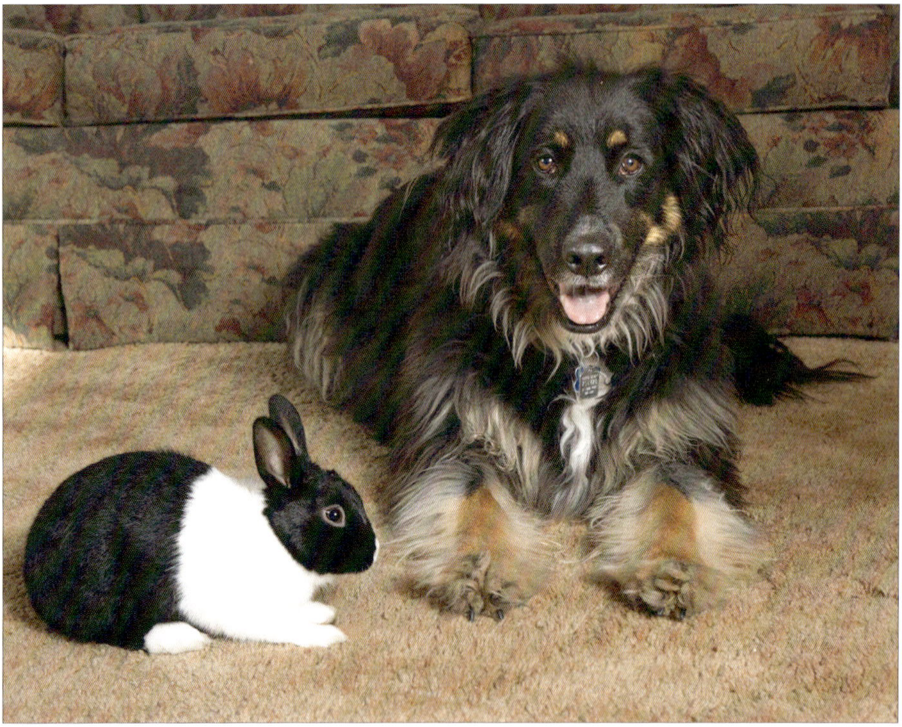

above:
Cujo shares his home with three cats, two birds, and a rabbit named Wesley. Also known as "the Ref," Cujo settles disputes over food and he often defends Wesley from marauding cats.

opposite:
Teeny is so tiny that she can fit comfortably in an old cowboy boot.

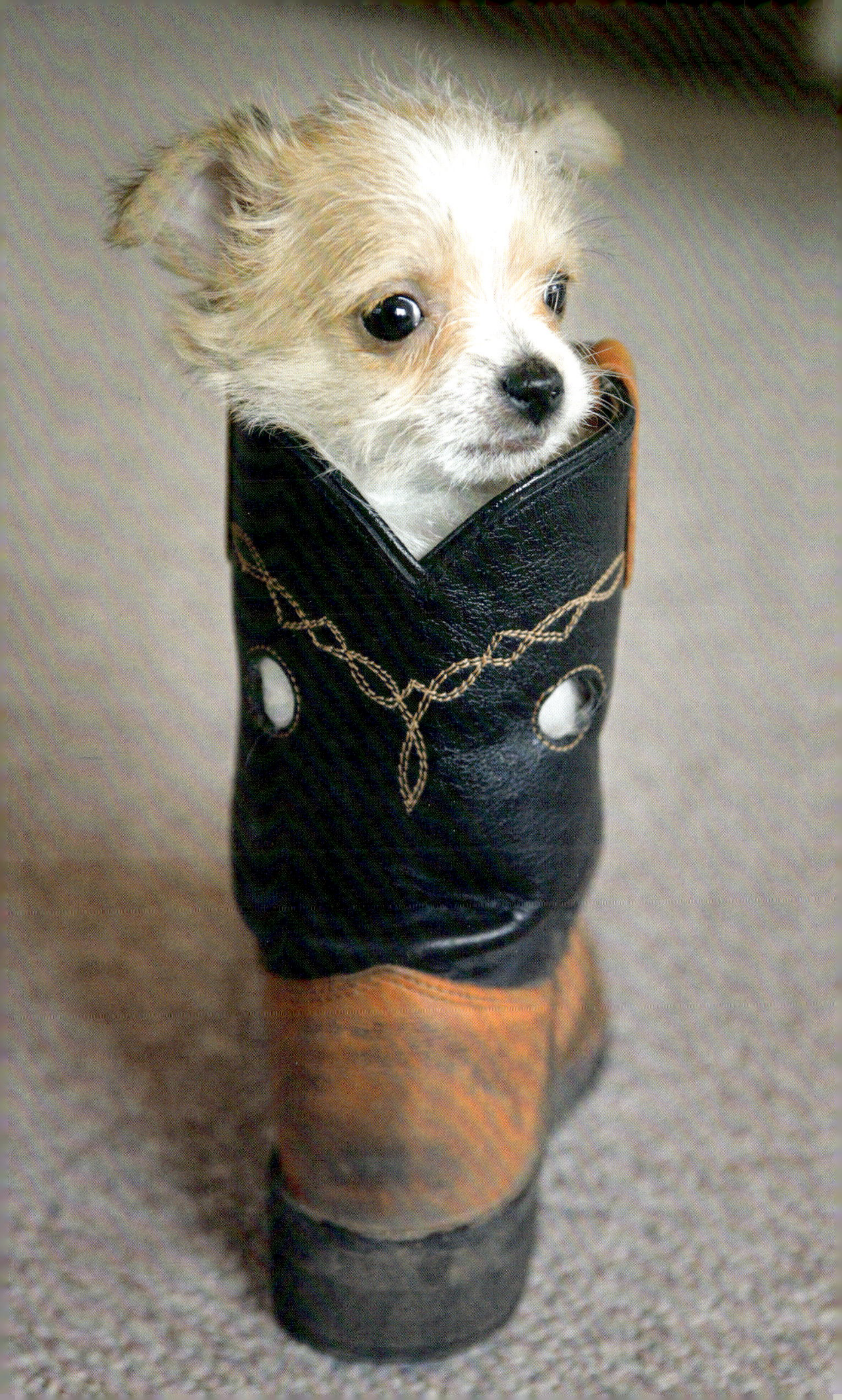

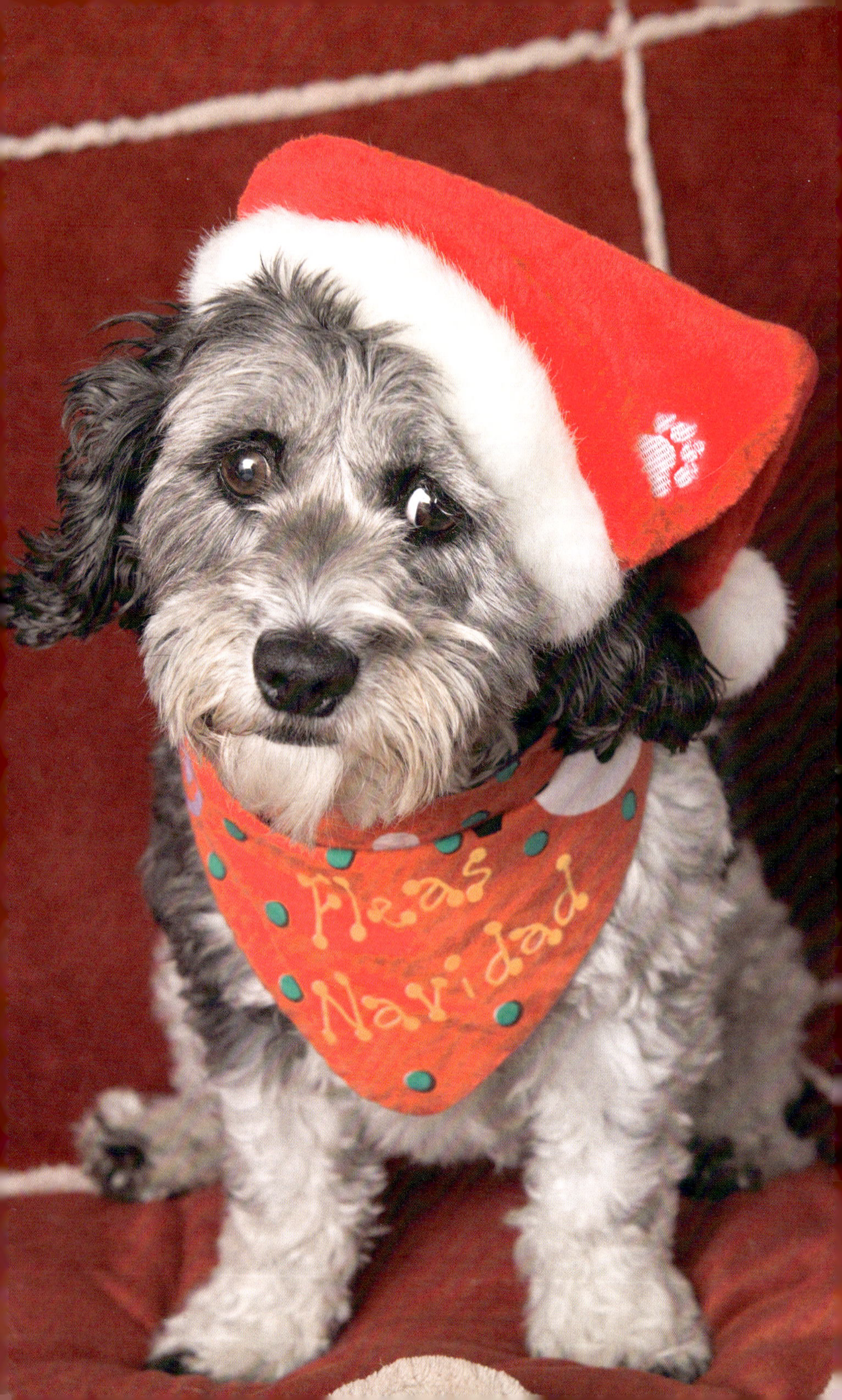
Fleas Navidad

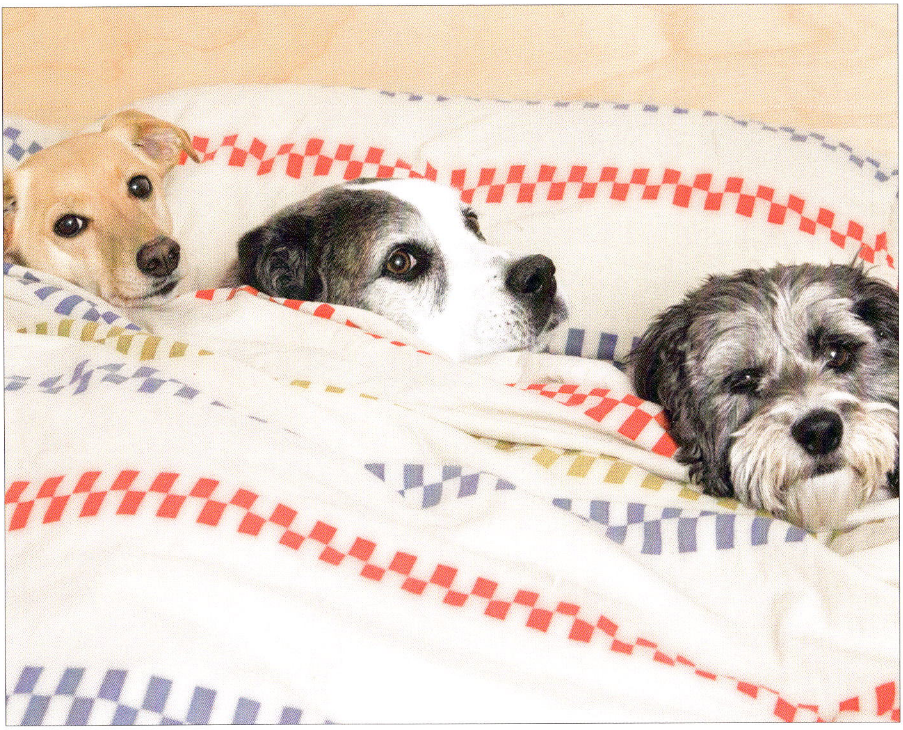

opposite:
Abby is the life of the Christmas party. She is even willing to share the snacks from her stocking.

above:
Frankie, Casey, and Abby enjoy cuddling. When their owner gets up in the morning, these three little rascals jump right in to take advantage of a warm bed.

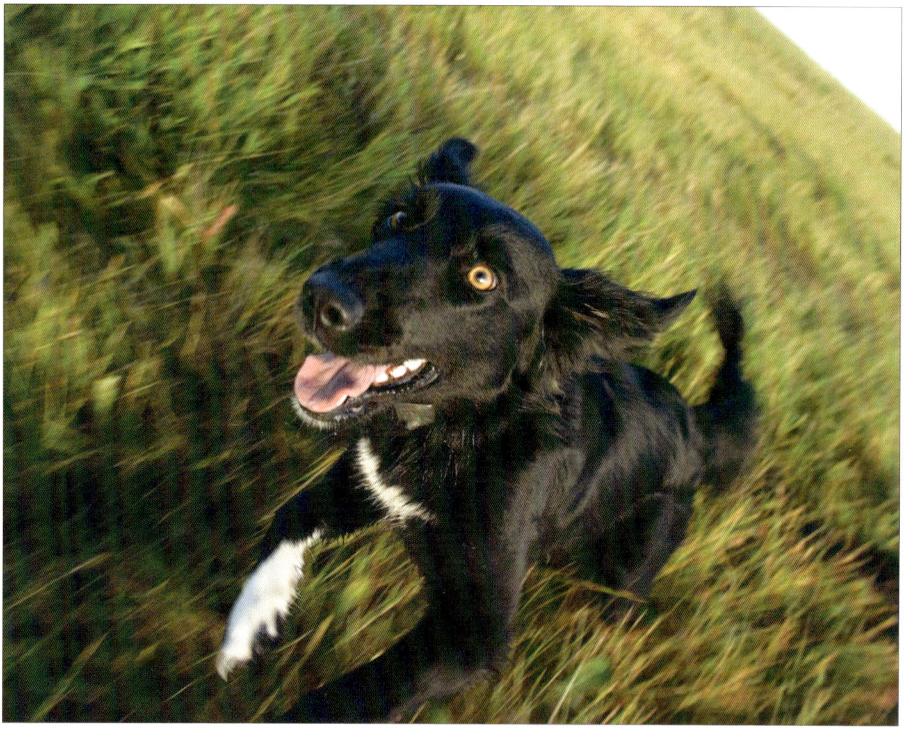

above:
Tess's face reveals the pure joy of a romp in the field.

opposite:
Tuk loves to catch anything you throw at him — including small rocks! For this photo session, Tuk displayed his midair catch technique.

pages 20–21:
Allie's agility and prowess are remarkable: a mere 40 centimetres (14 in) tall, she can jump about 1 metre (40 in) off the ground.

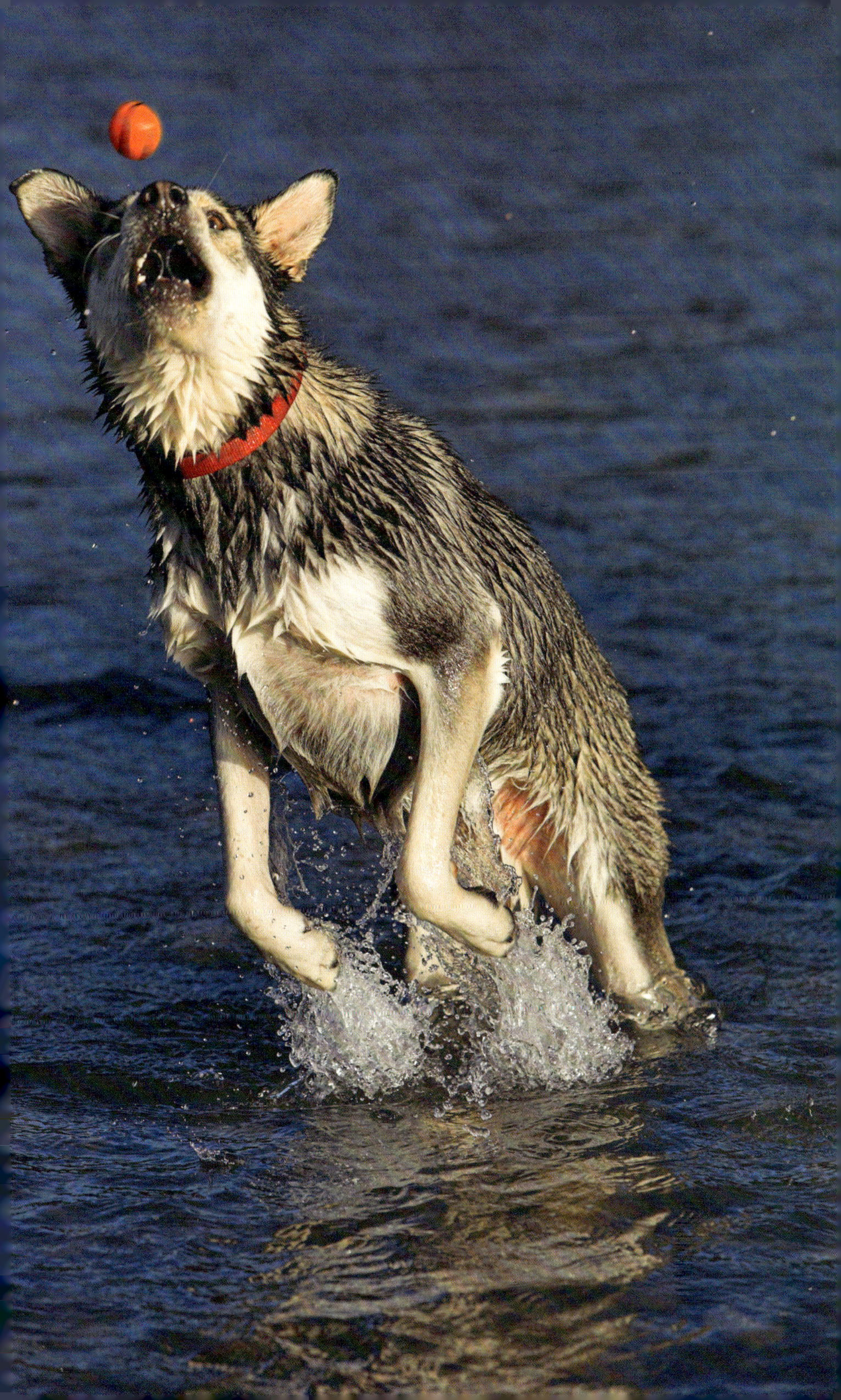

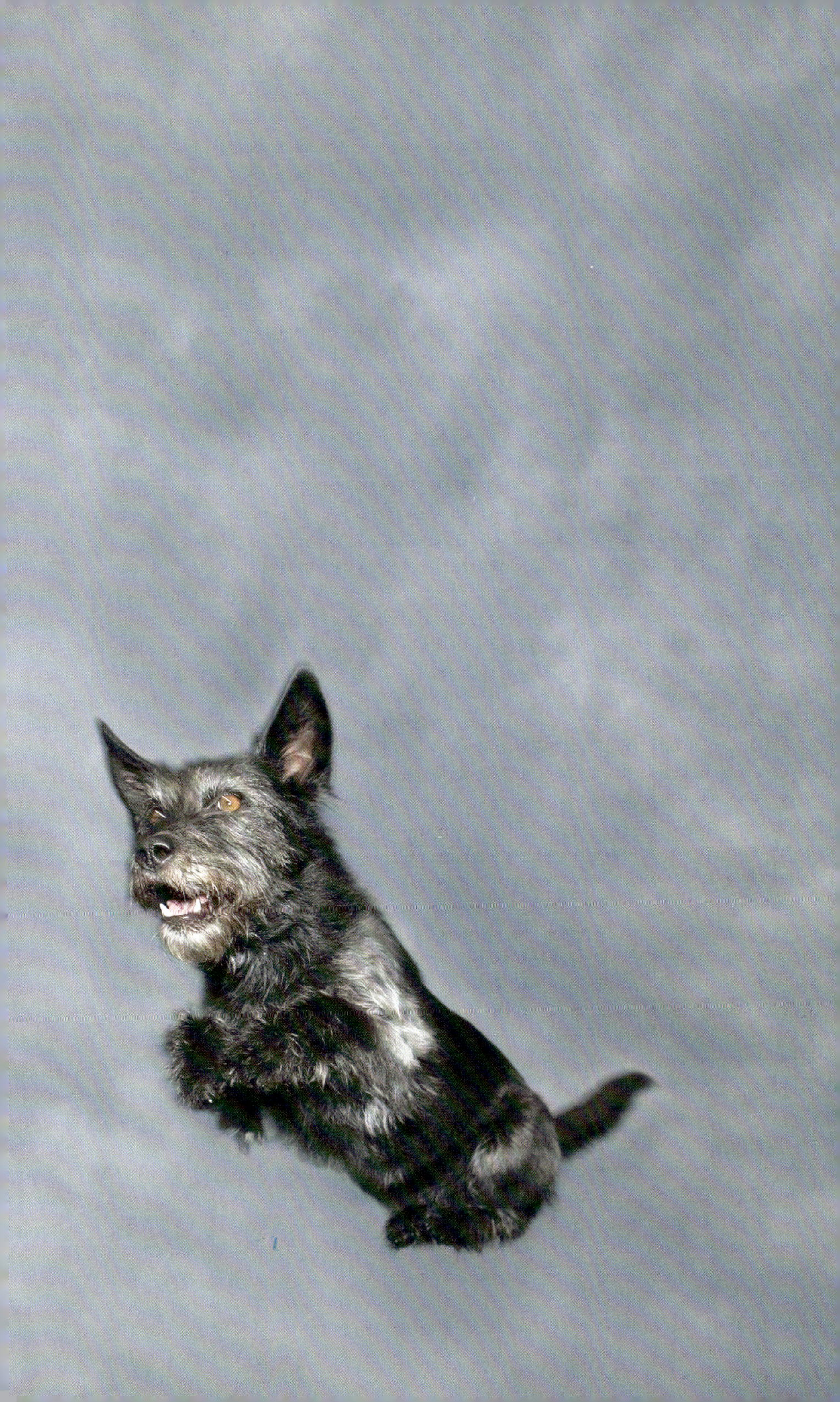

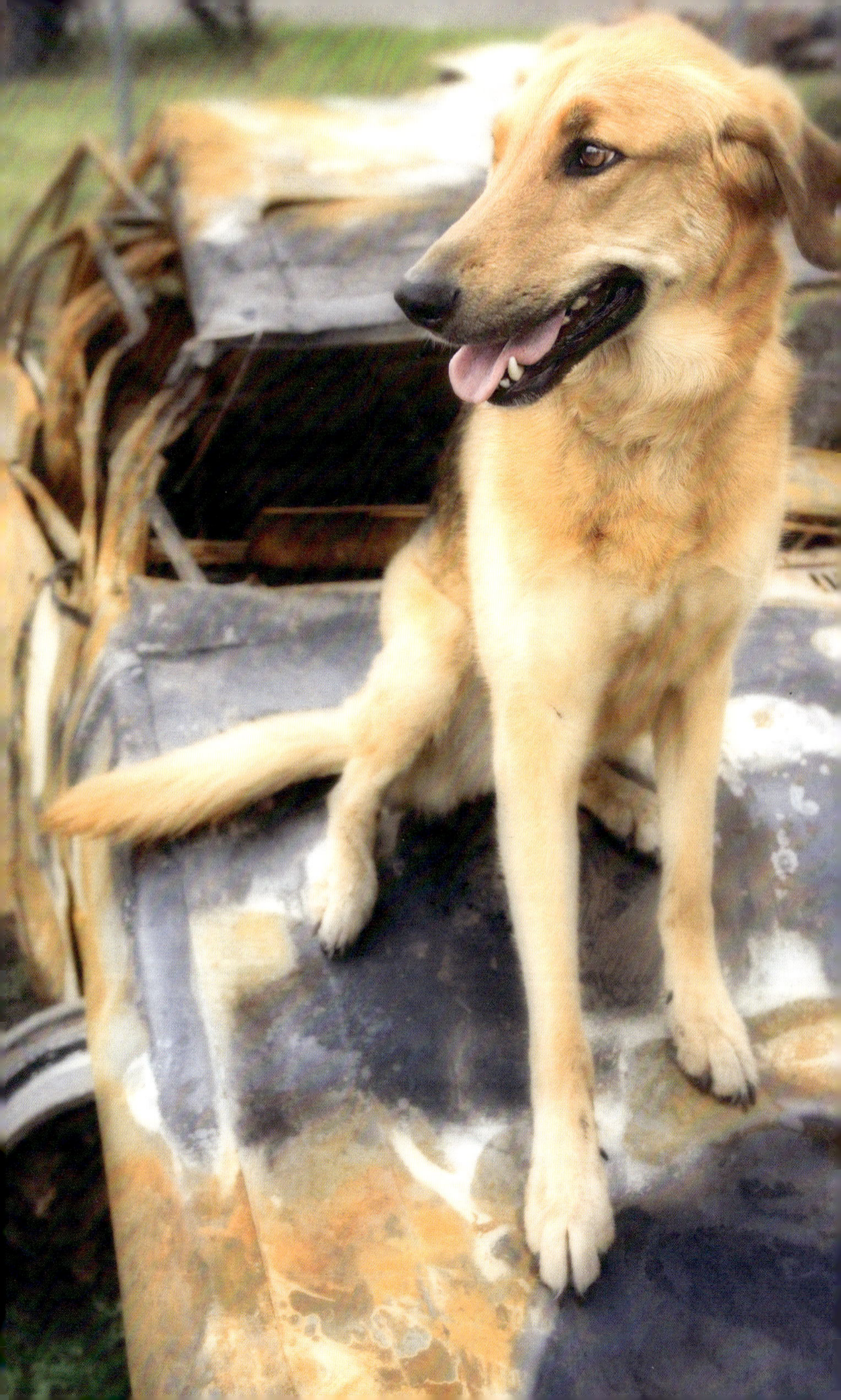

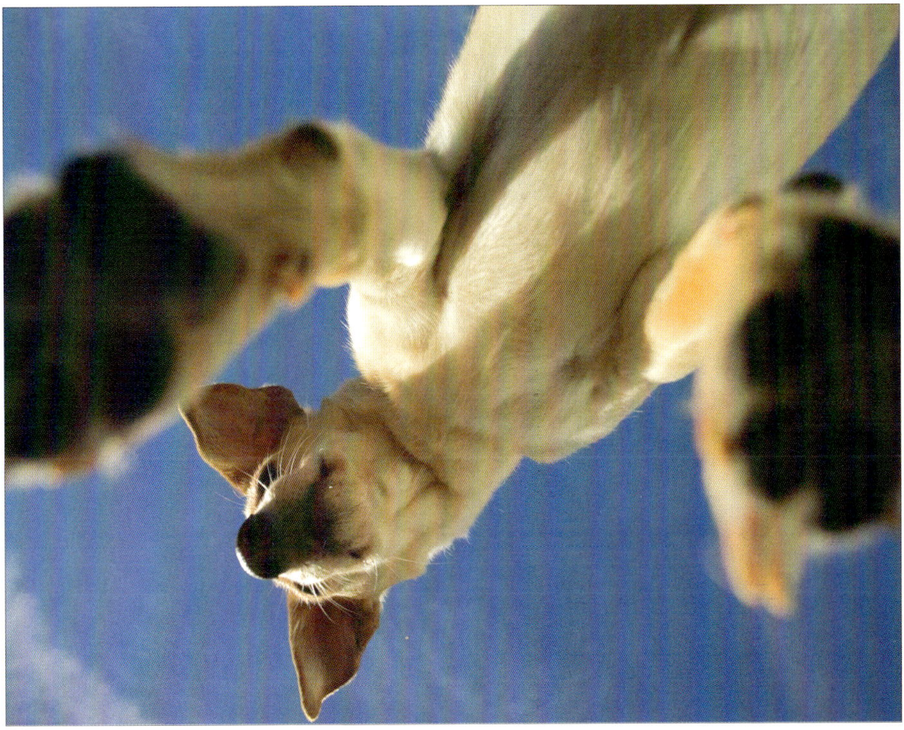

opposite:
A junkyard dog, Cola is a greyhound cross that likes to tease other dogs by bumping them with her nose and then running away.

above:
This photograph of Frankie was taken from beneath his owner's glass coffee table.

page 24:
Milo is a patient introvert. He will wait on the deck for hours for something exciting to happen — such as a ride in the truck!

page 25:
Leroy was a skinny, one-year-old stray, who had been shot in the face, when he was found wandering the streets. Now, he is a healthy, happy dog who loves to wear his owner's clothes.

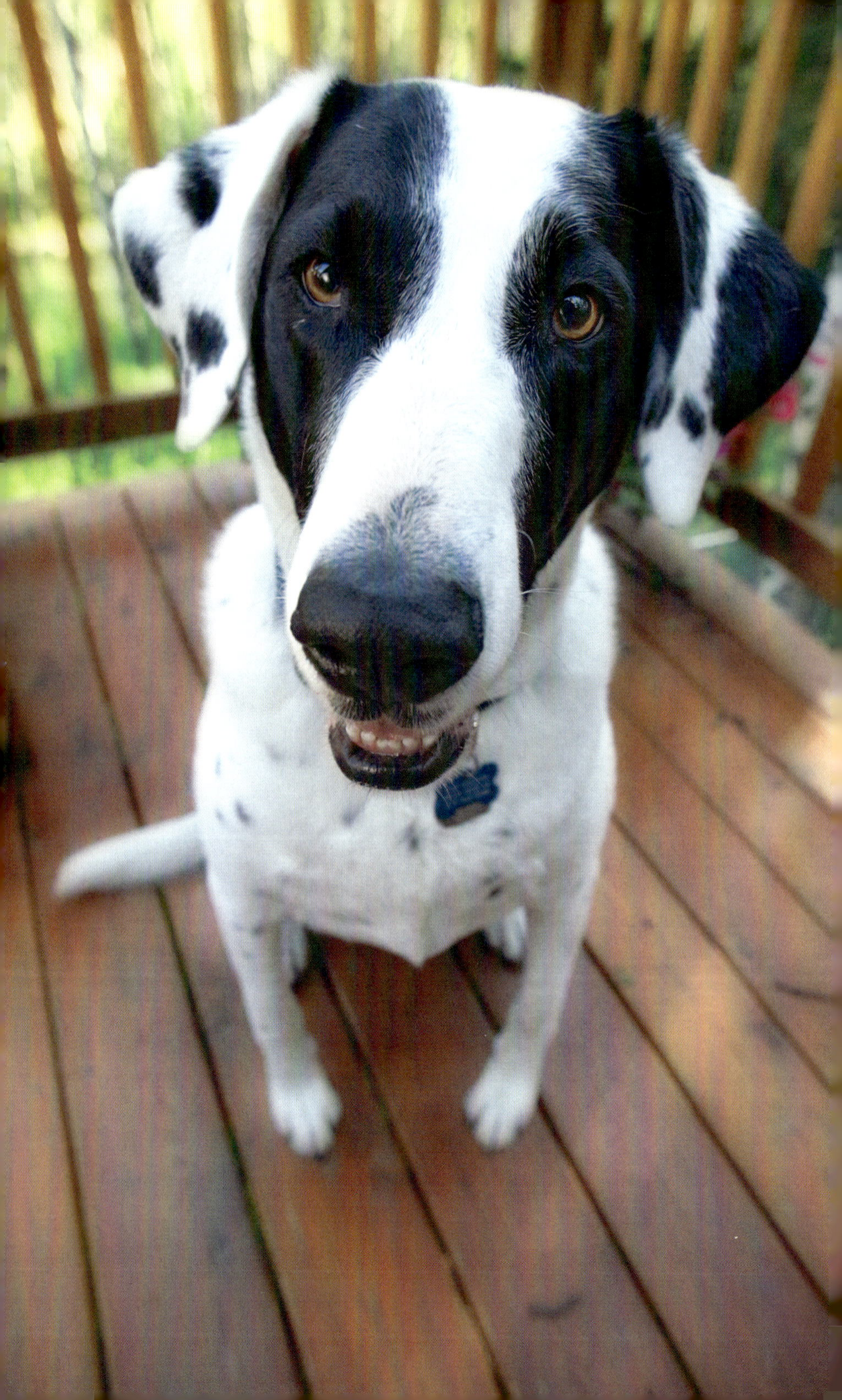

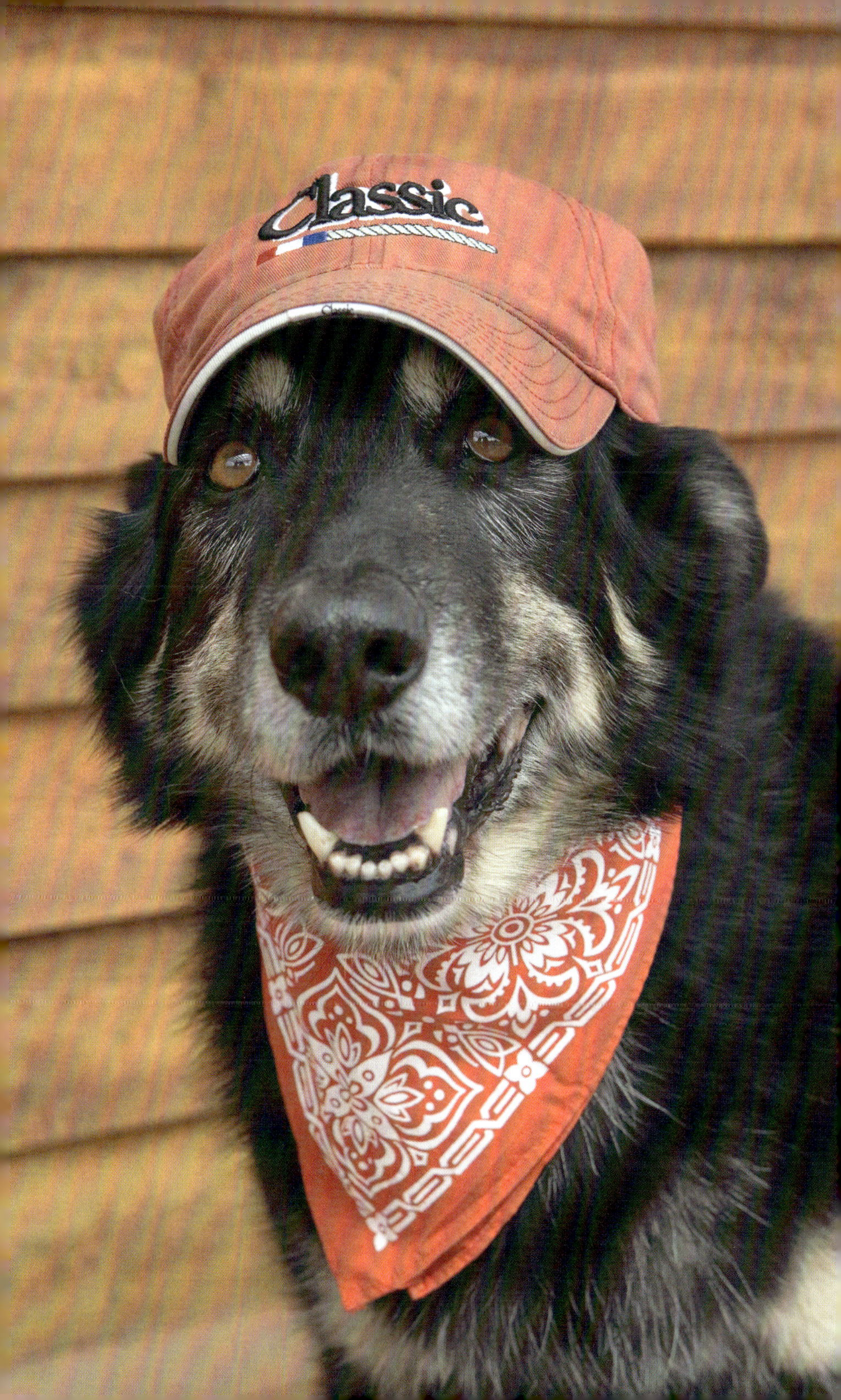
Classic

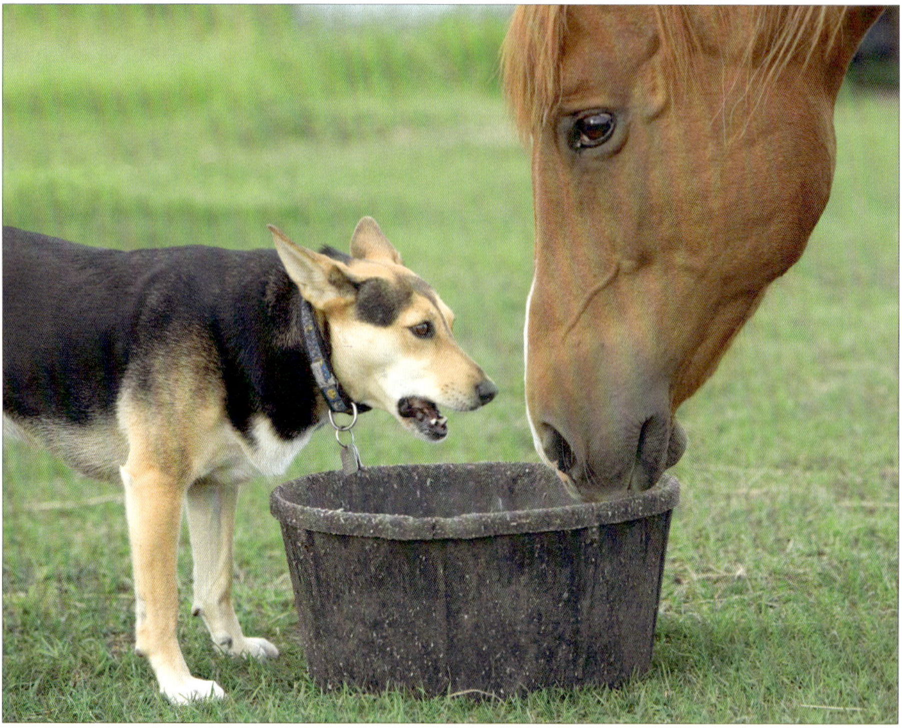

above:
Annie loves horse pellets. Luckily, her equine neighbour does not mind sharing them with her.

opposite:
Grymm is really playful. New friends can tell when he is happy because his teeth chatter non-stop.

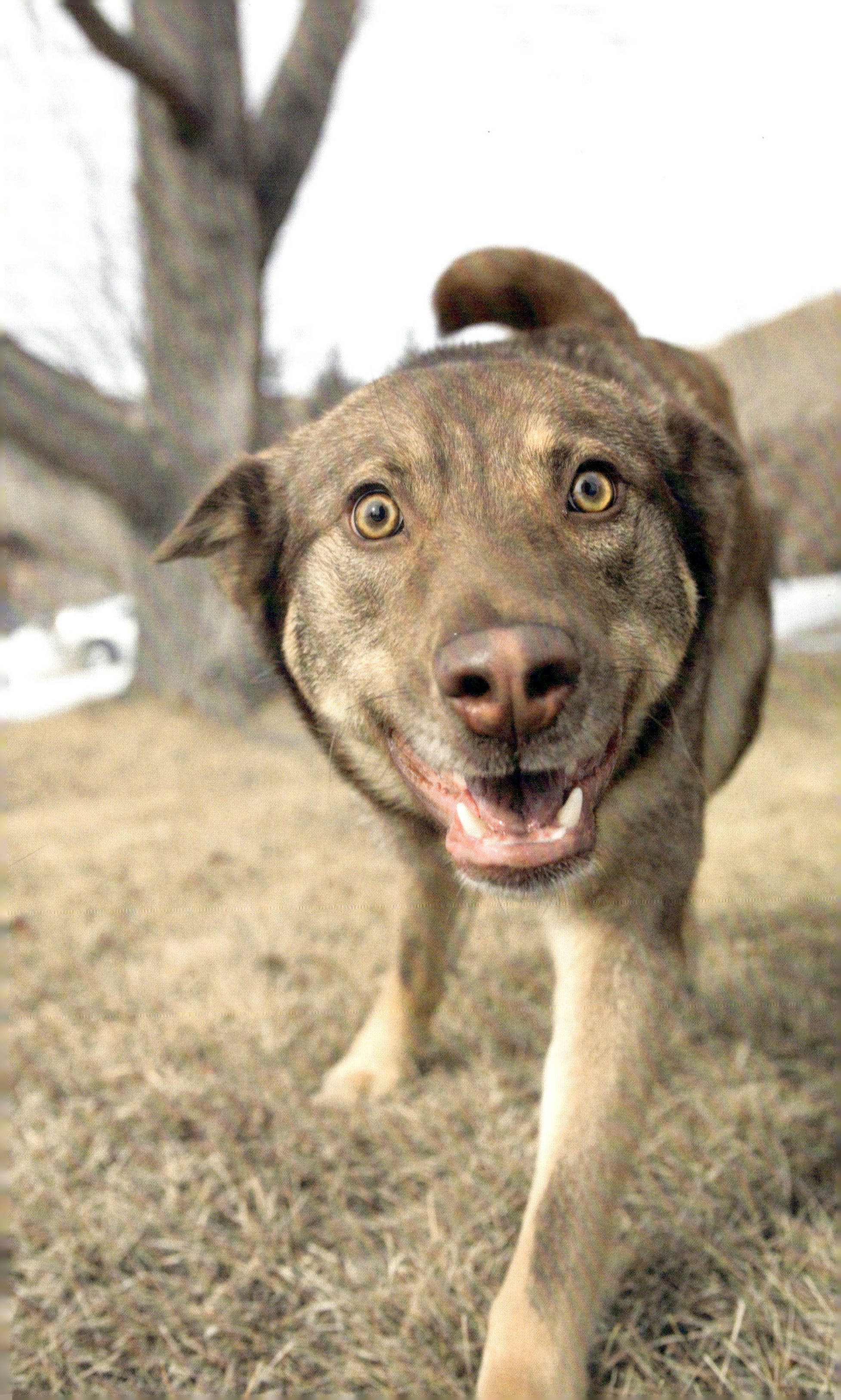

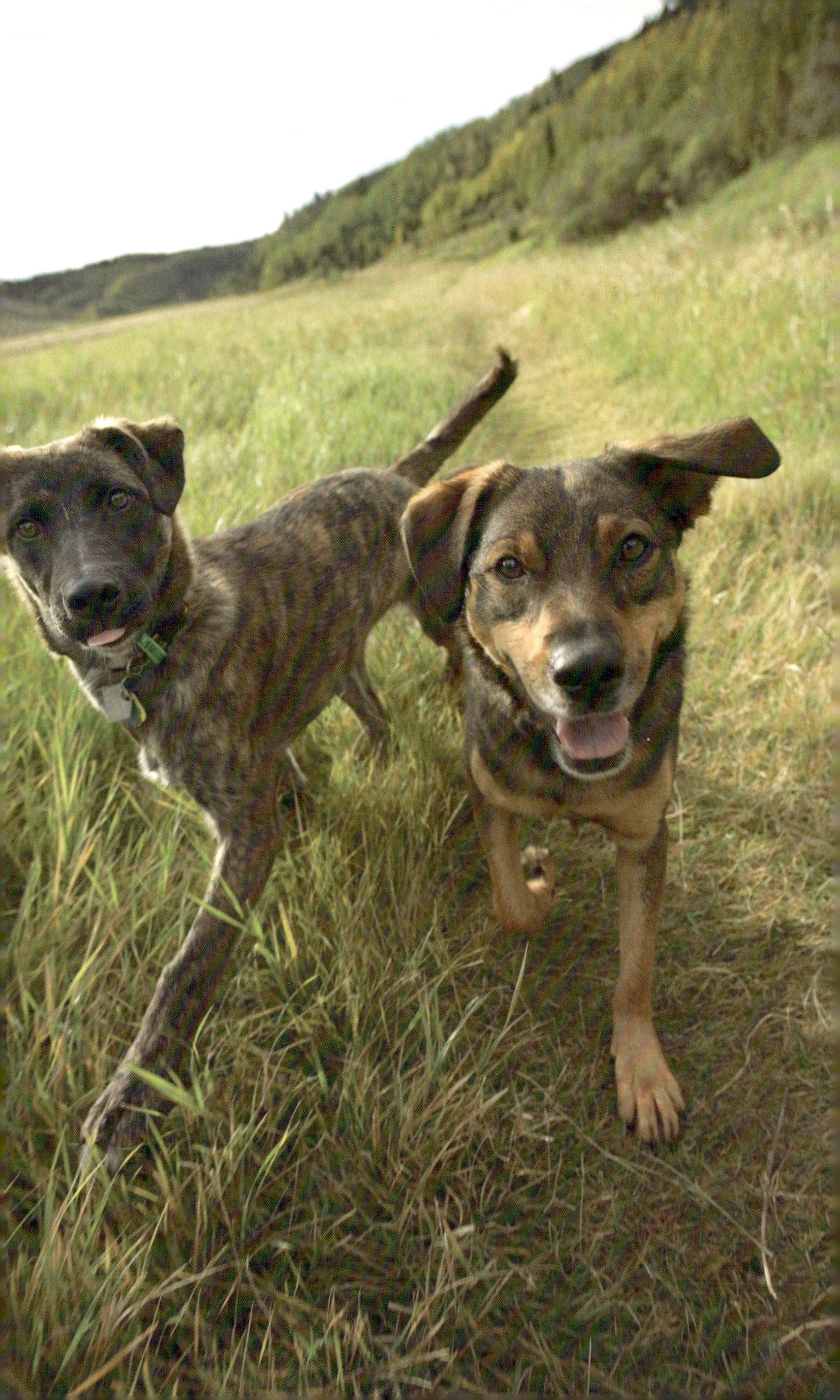

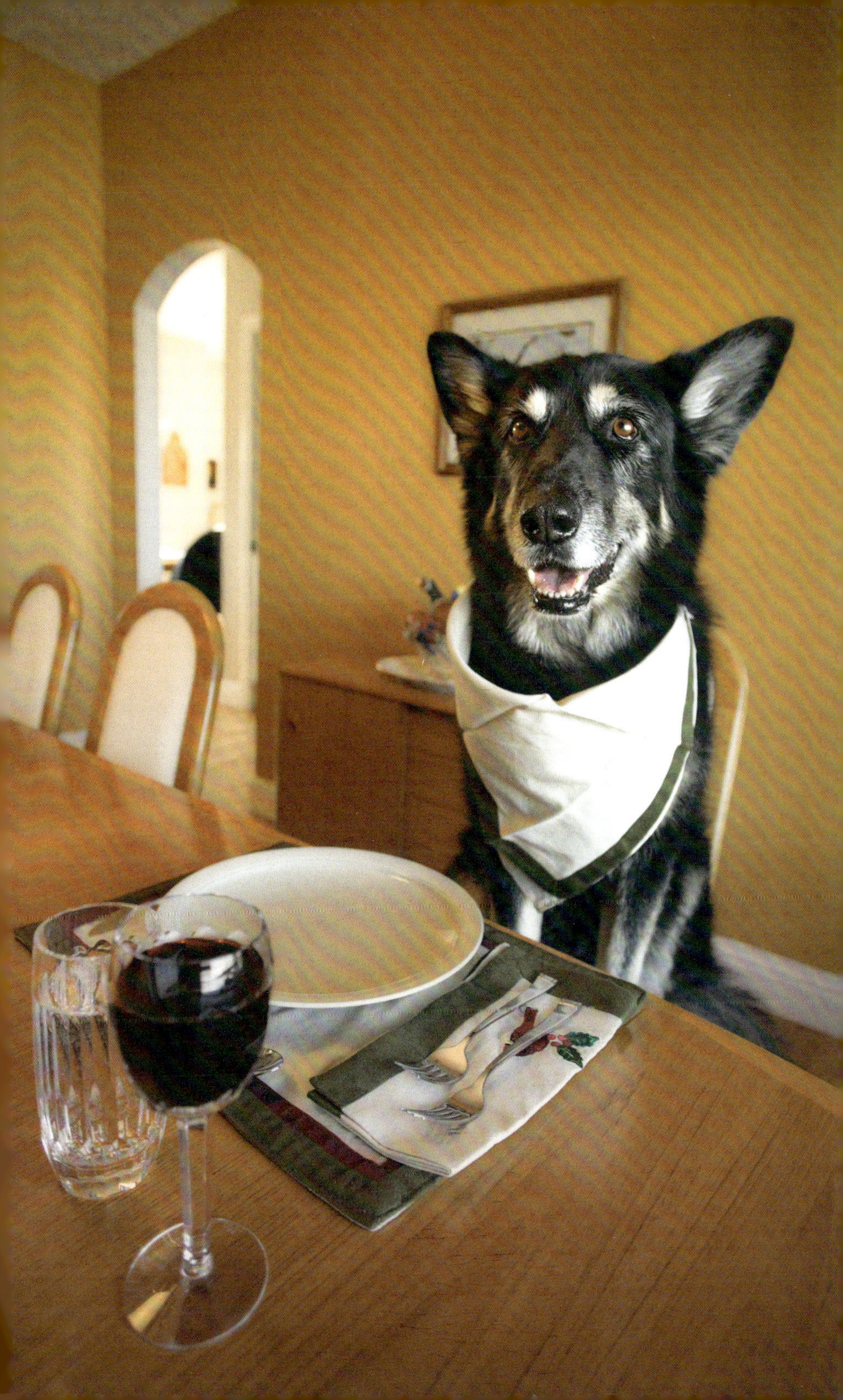

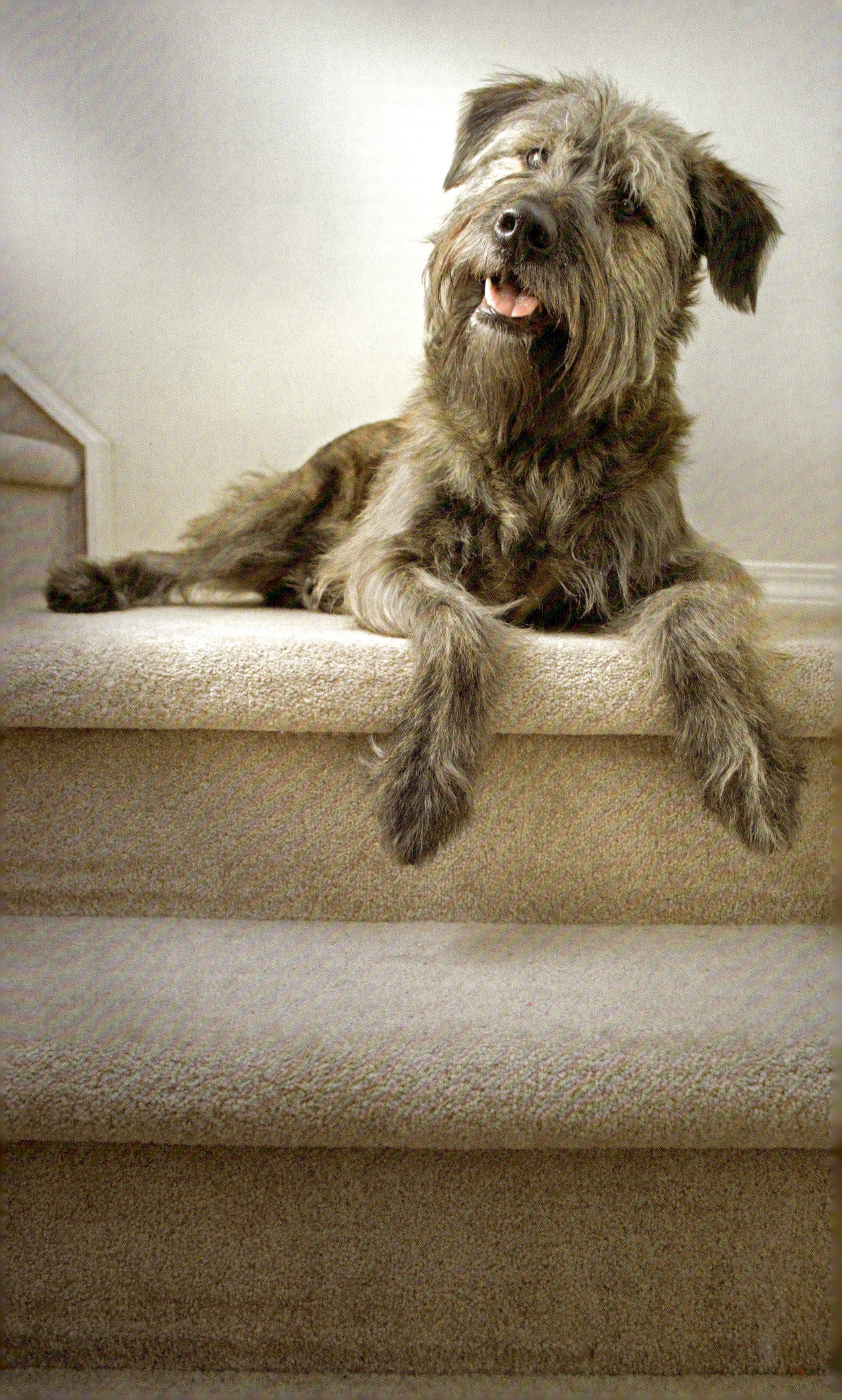

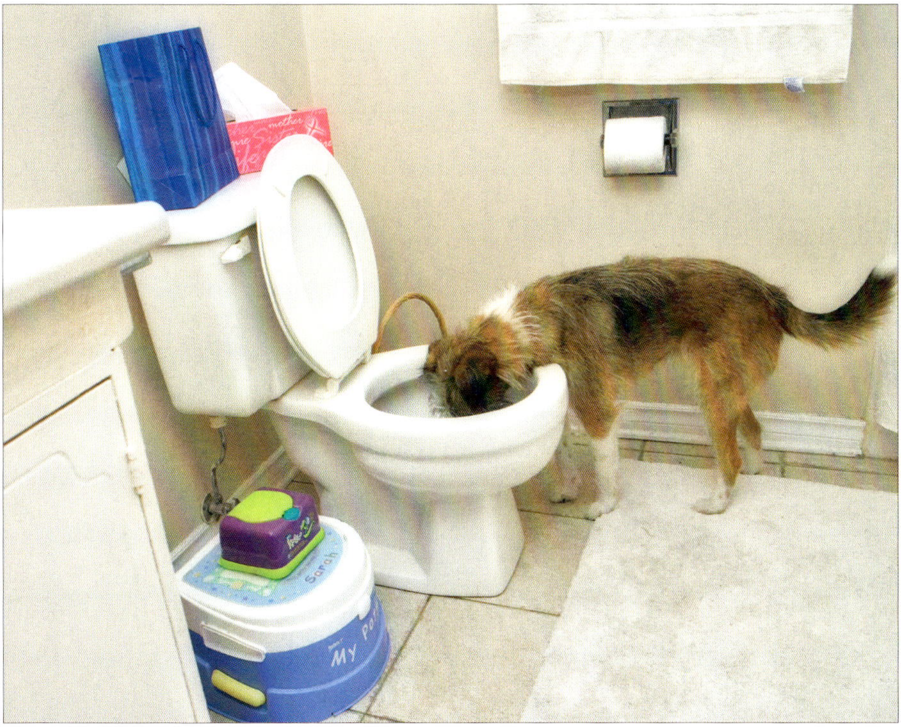

opposite:
As a puppy, Jackson was known as "Tank" because of his size and clumsiness. He now weighs 65 pounds, but he firmly believes he's a lap dog, much to the surprise of visitors.

above:
Murphy enjoys one of the privileges of being a dog — discovering the magic well.

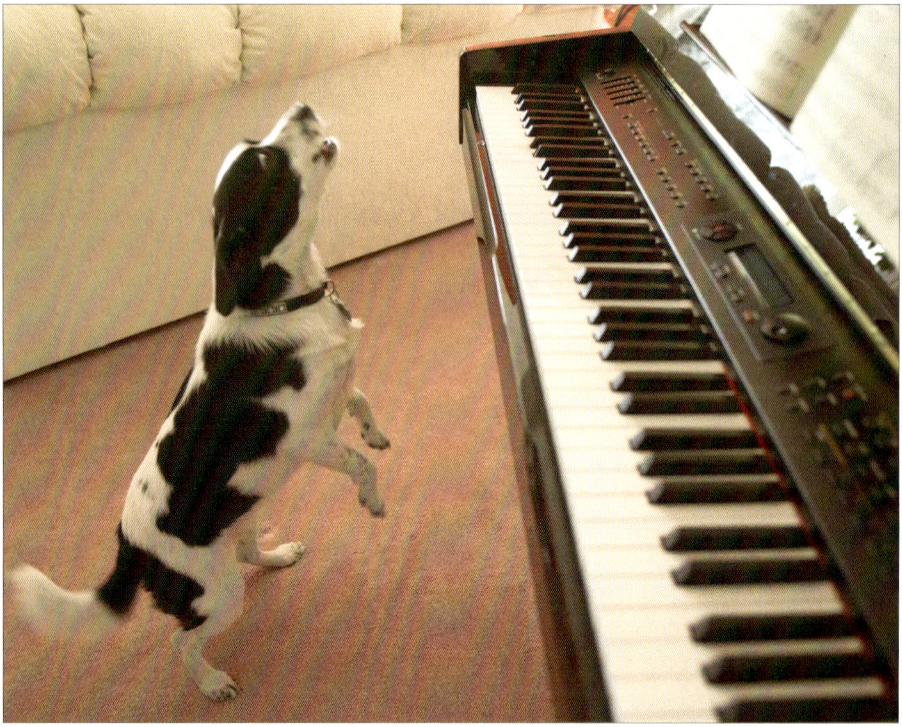

above:
Also known as "Princess," Prada runs the household. In this photo, she demands a little after-snack entertainment.

opposite:
Mayu loves to howl. When her owners start up, she is quick to join in.

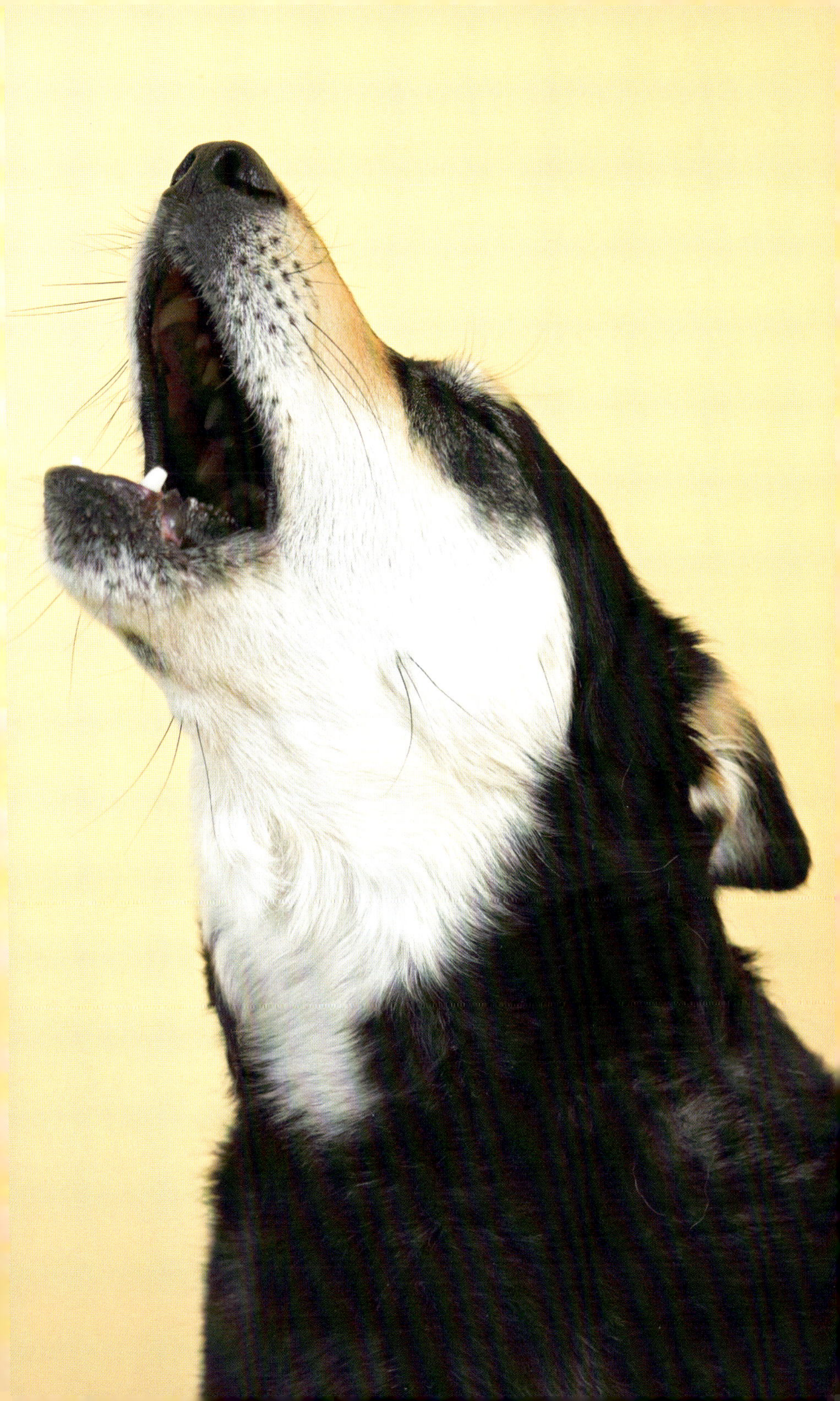

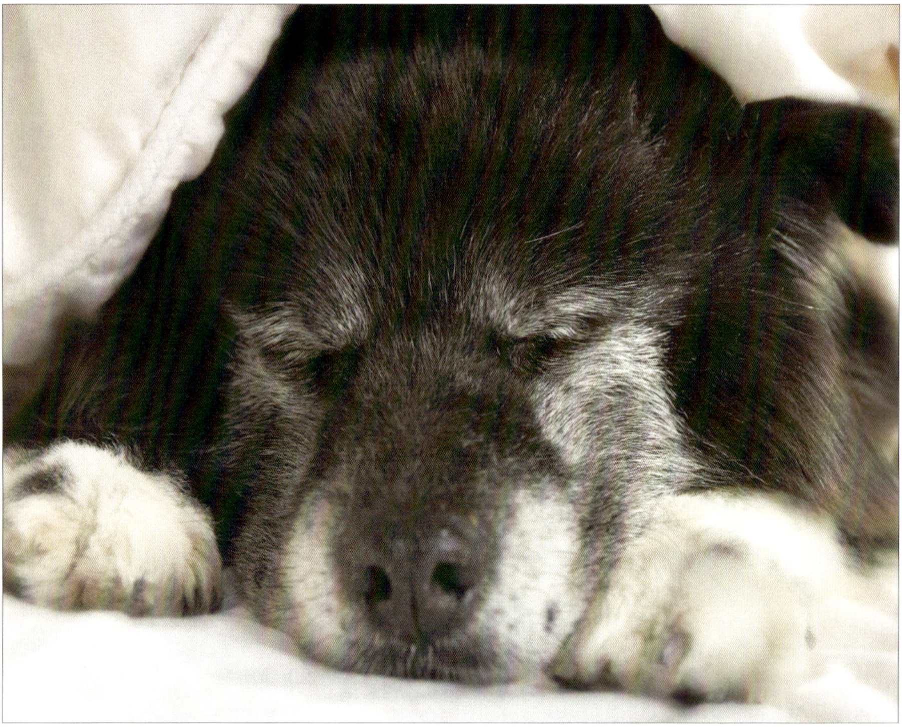

above:
Rescued at age three, Casey was a Newfoundland–Samoyed cross whose sole purpose was to love and be loved. He became a therapy dog. He helped people with severe depression and those suffering from Alzheimer's. Casey passed away at age 15, just weeks after this photo was taken.

opposite:
In this photo, Harley is in his element. He has a relaxed attitude to life.

pages 38–39:
When Lika disapproves, she flattens her ears. In this photo, her ears betray her feelings about the camera lens just inches from her nose.

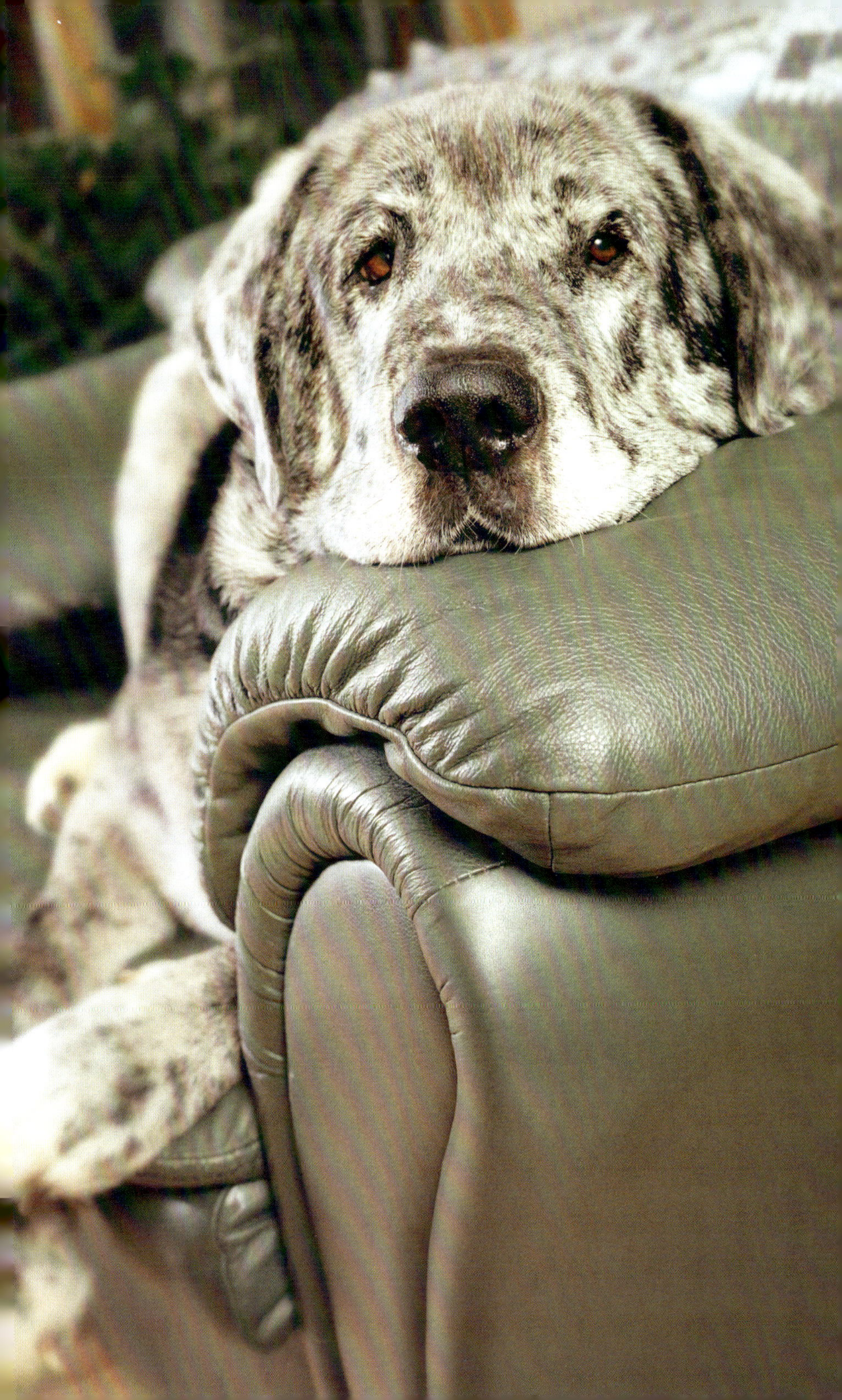

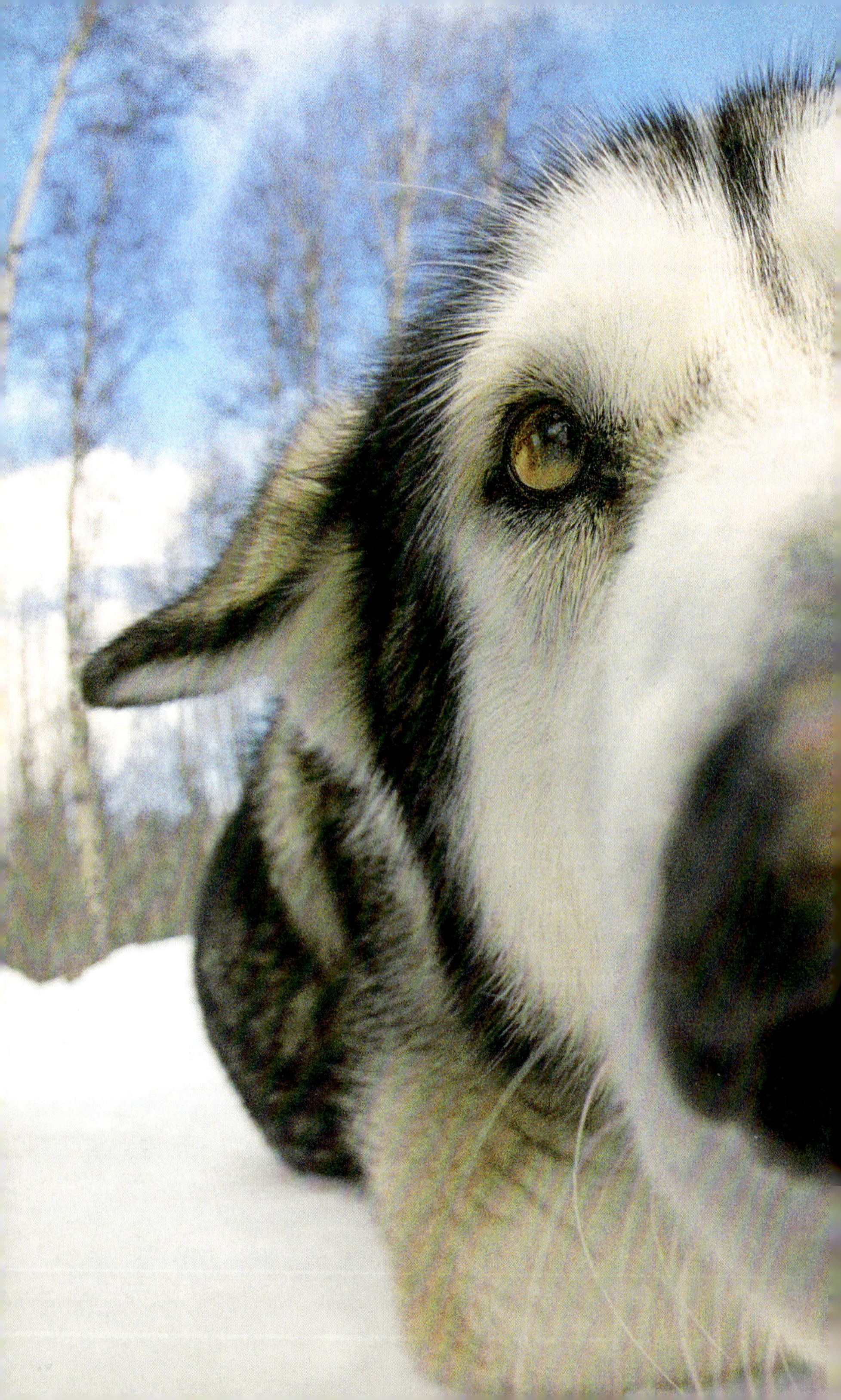

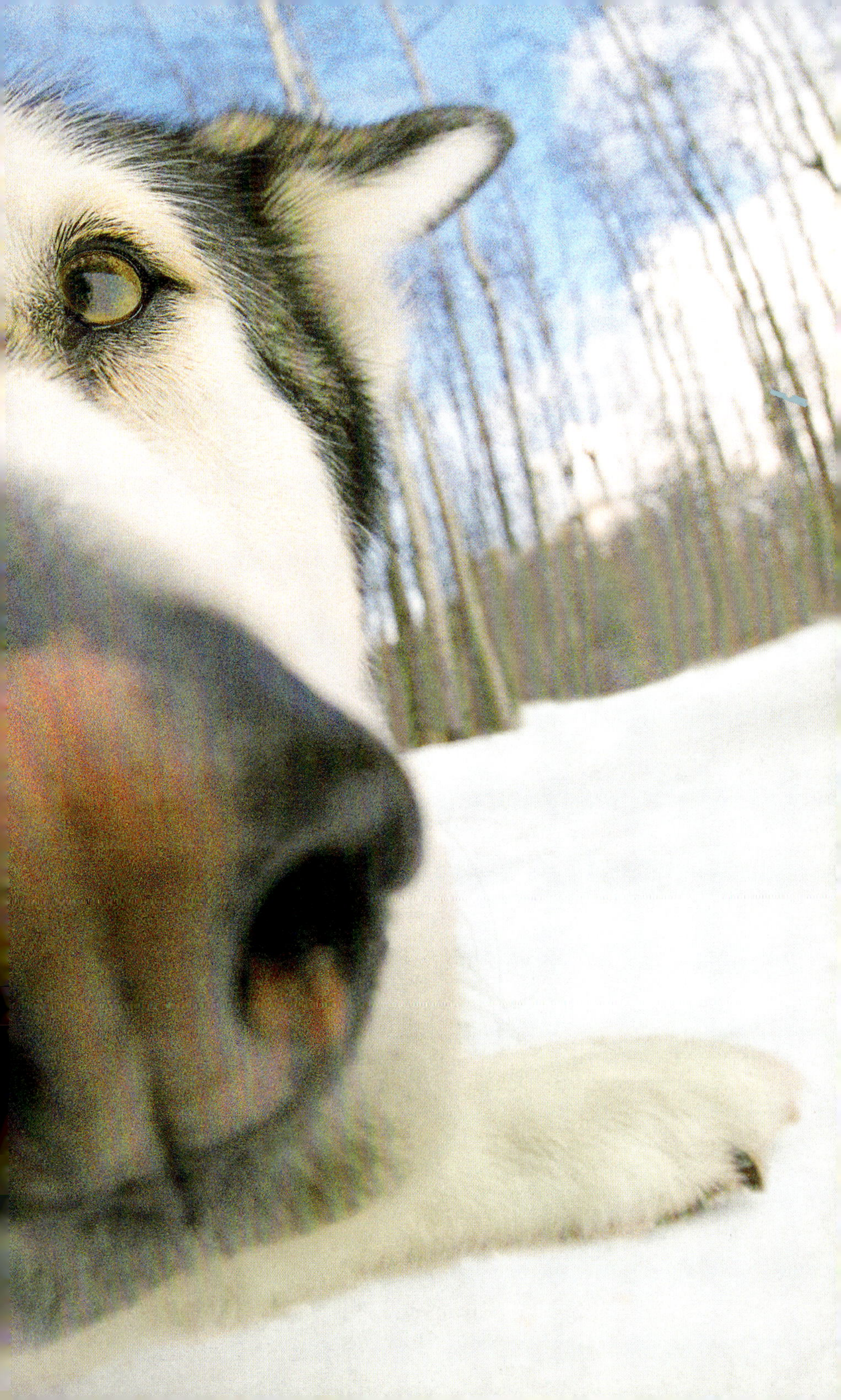

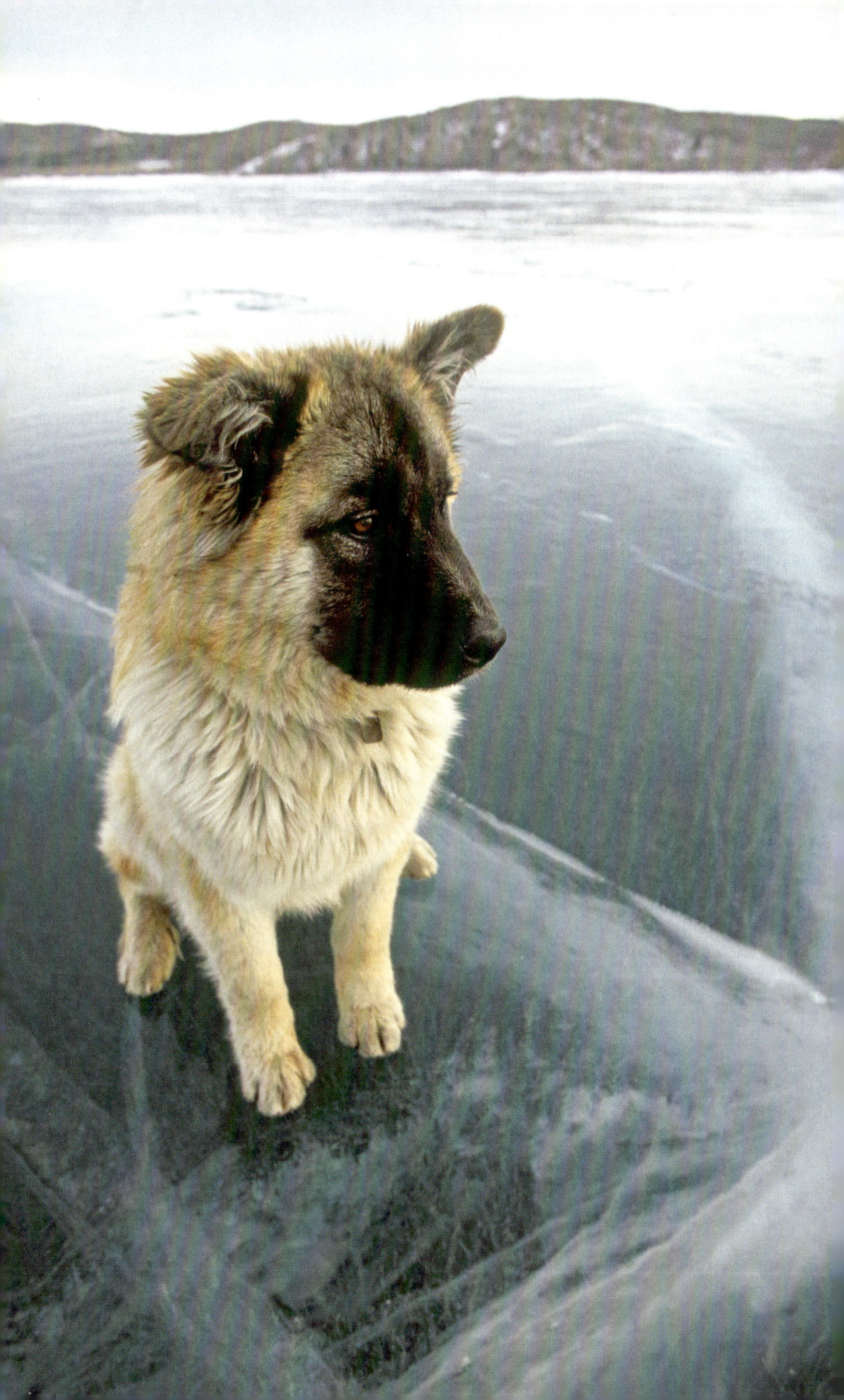

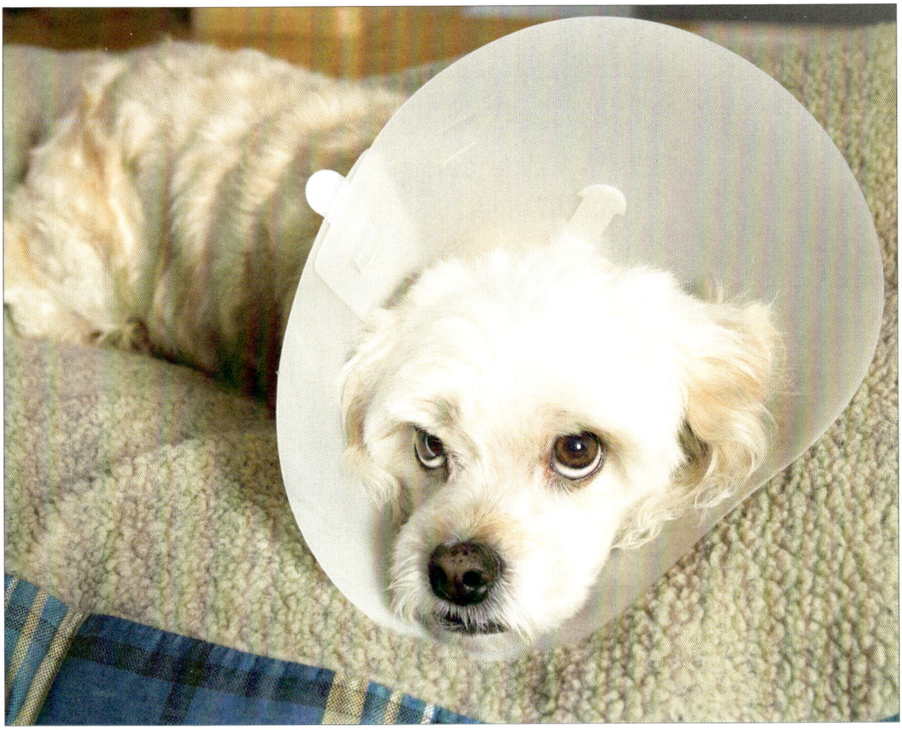

opposite:
Bear was a stray when she was found. Now, she is a working dog taking care of three girls. She has become very protective of her little charges.

above:
Normally a happy little dog, Sadie loves to please — except when she is forced to wear "the cone of humiliation."

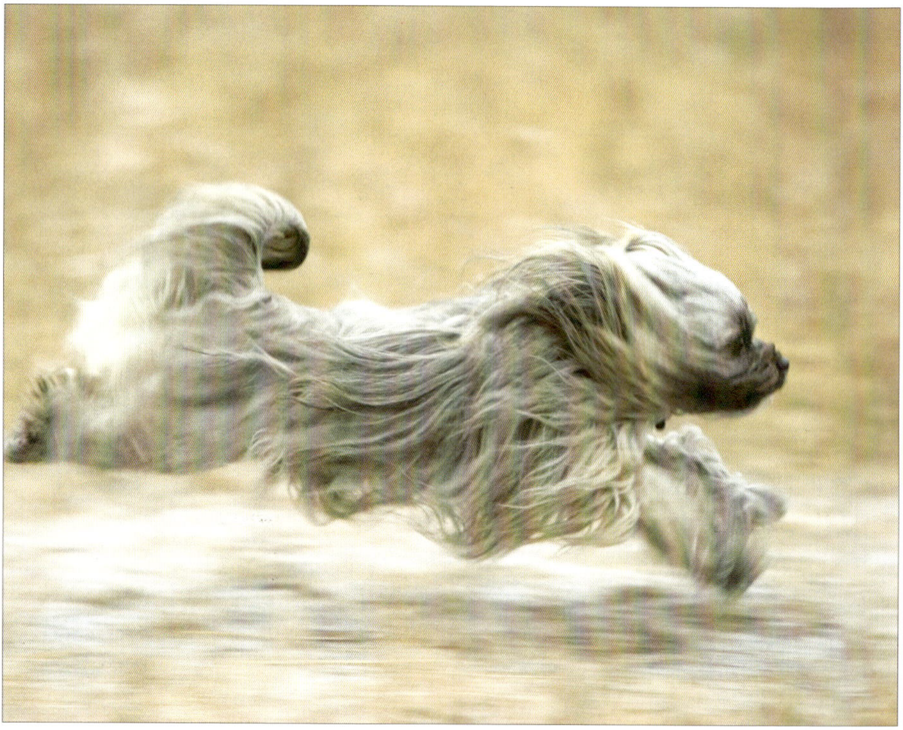

above:
Benny bounds enthusiastically toward his owner in anticipation of a treat.

opposite:
Nikita's owner spent a great deal of time blow-drying her dog's coat into a carefully fluffed coif before this photo was taken. But her handiwork was soon destroyed in a game of fetch in the river.

page 44:
The smell of freshly baked cookies is irresistable. Logan samples the goods when his owners are not looking.

page 45:
Lotse is well-mannered — she knows that the food on the table is off limits to four-legged friends.

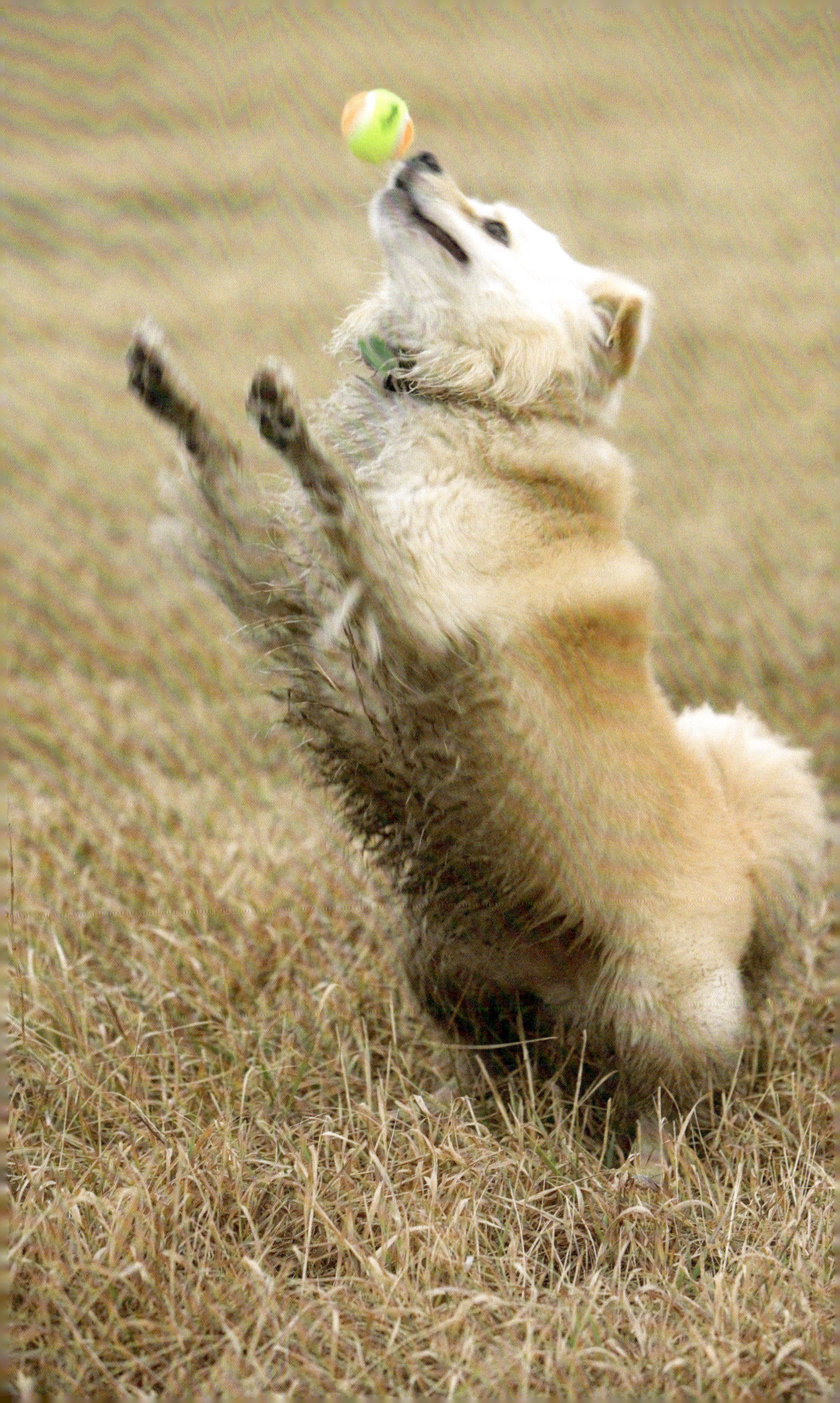

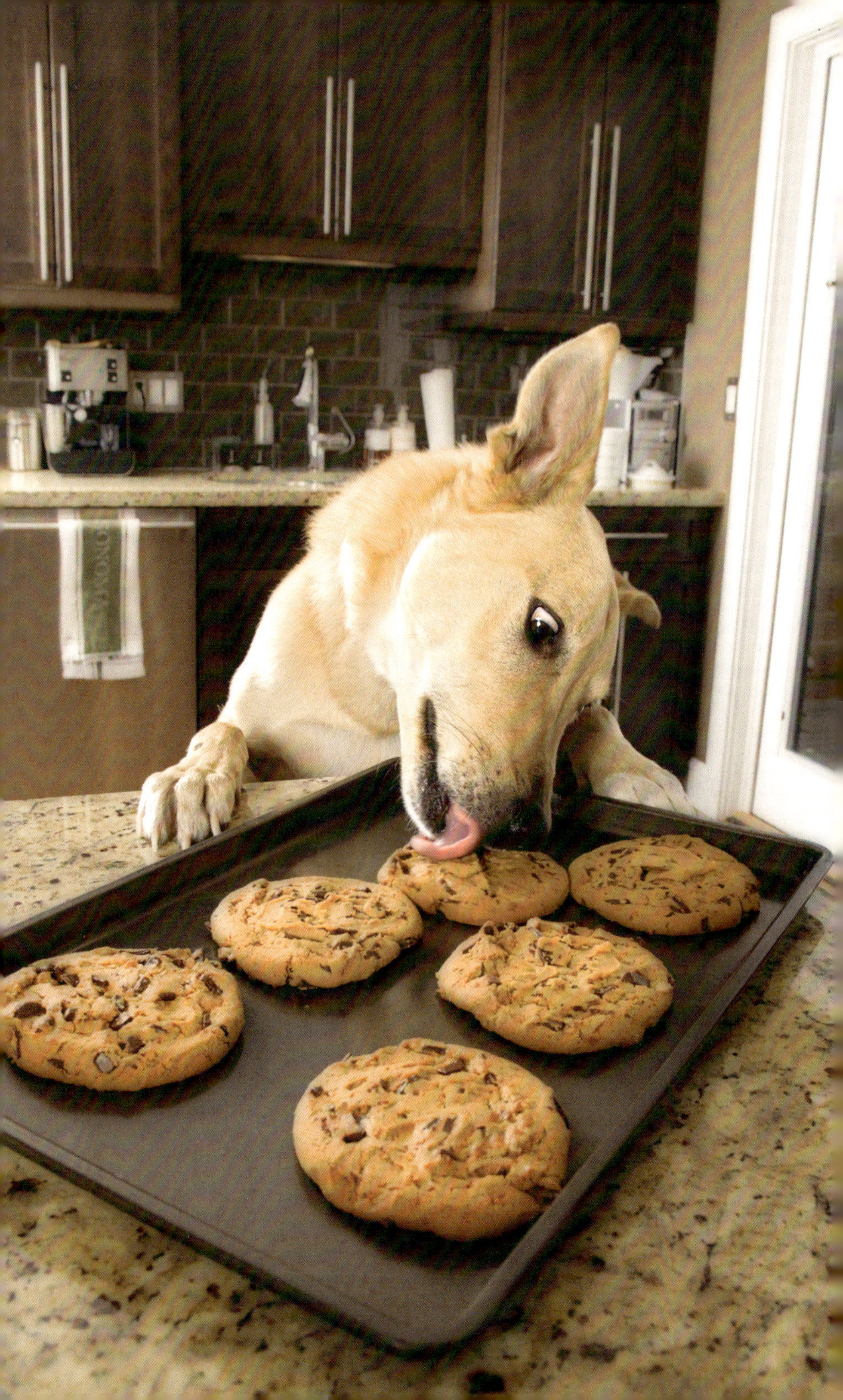

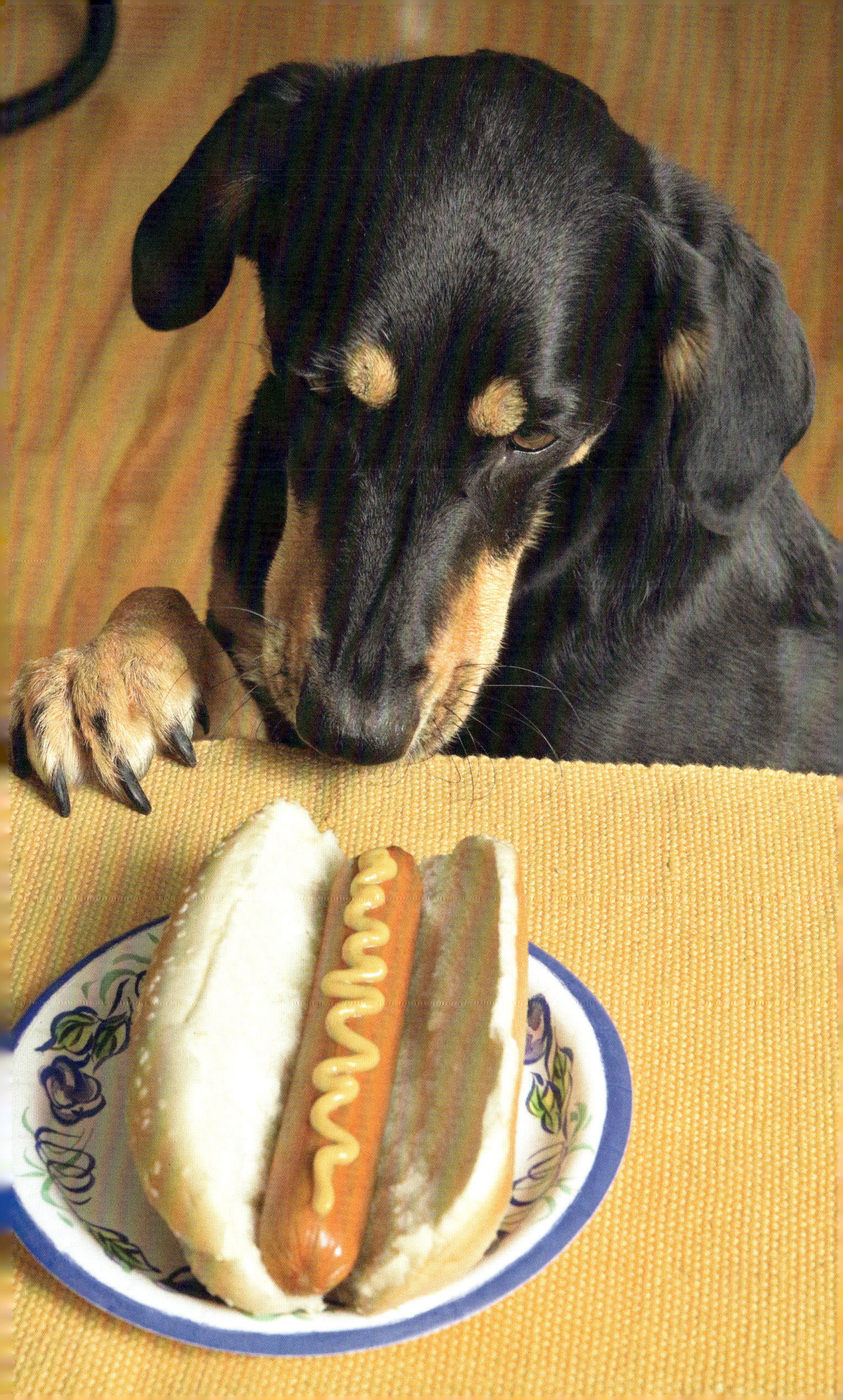

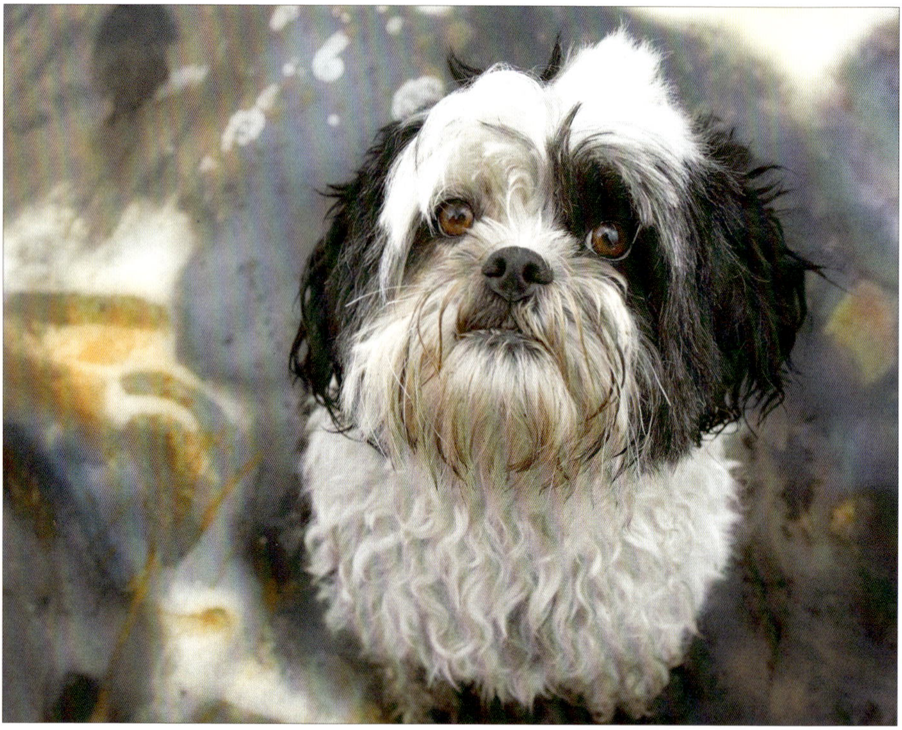

above:
Bronti helps Cola patrol the junkyard. Bronti often invites trespassers into the yard so that the pair of dogs can score free back rubs.

opposite:
Grymm realizes he has been busted.

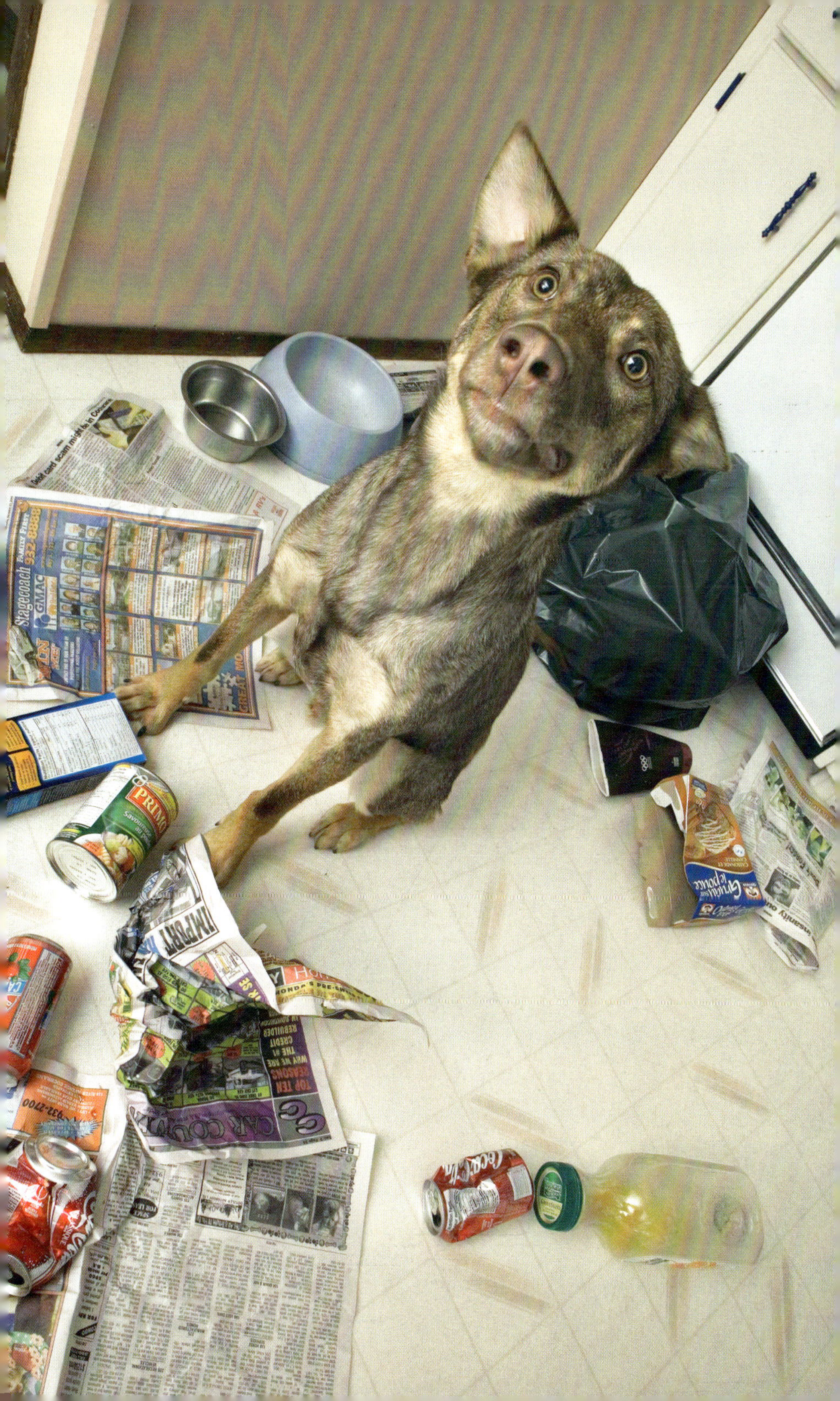
Stagecoach
GMAC
PRIMO

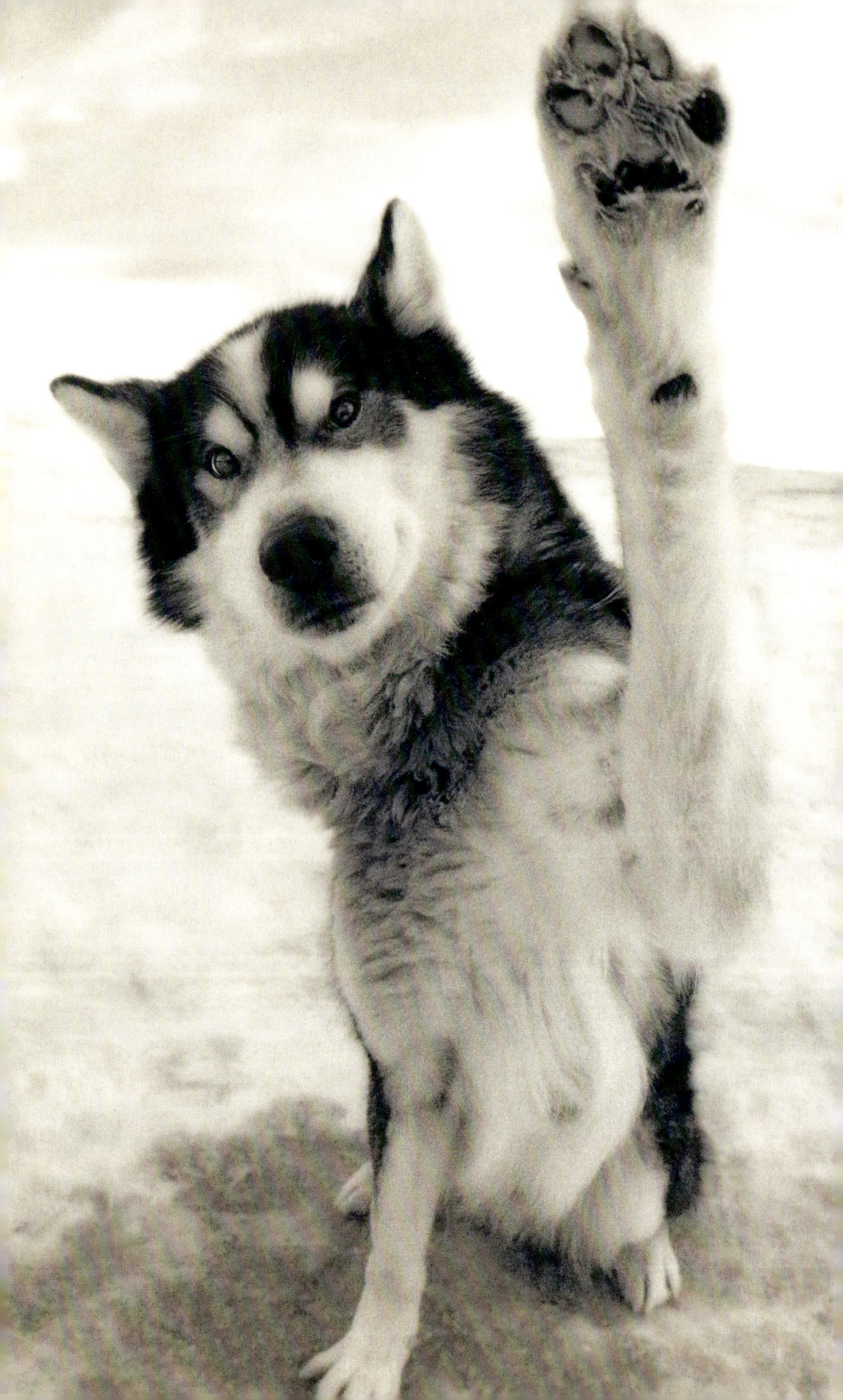

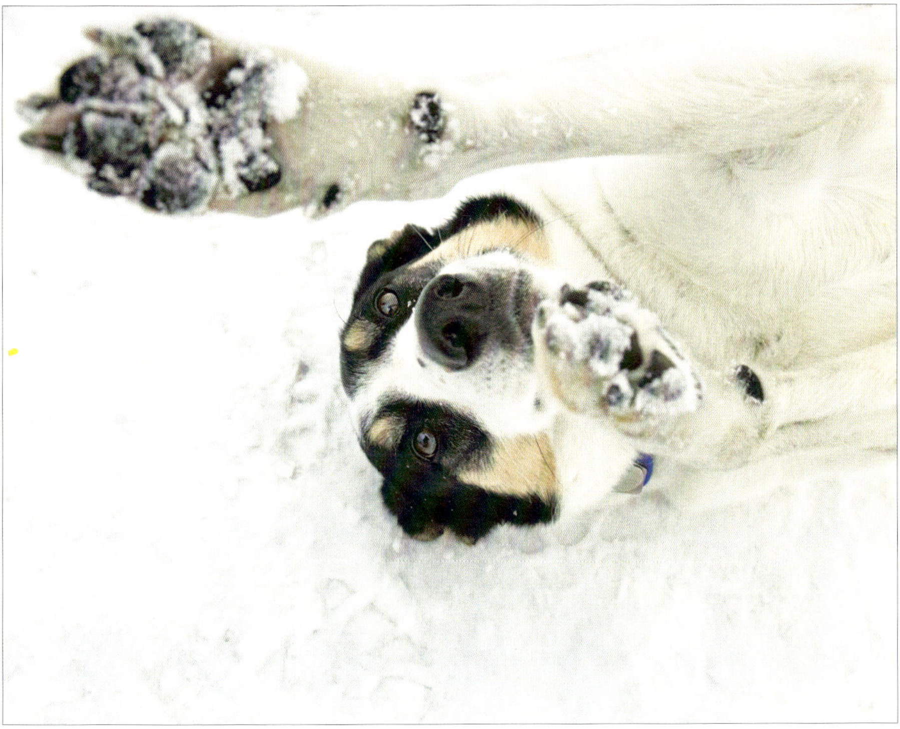

opposite:
A retired sled dog, Buster still raises a paw to signal his eagerness to be picked for the trip.

above:
When she greets new friends, Tess likes to roll on her back and give them a high five.

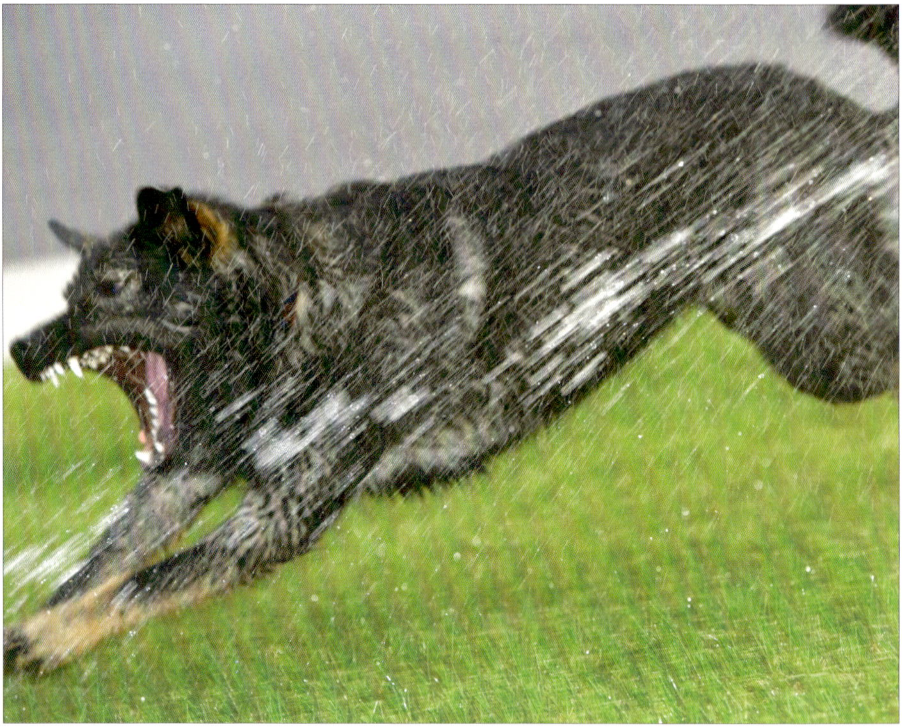

above:
Nyla's favourite game involves trying to kill the spray of water from the hose.

opposite:
Teak, right on the photographer's heels, was looking forward to the treats she knew were hidden in a pocket somewhere. Nothing gets past her!

page 52:
Desoto is a patient dog, smiling for the camera in his fashionable duds.

page 53:
Niko's casual "winter in Whistler" ensemble was a hit.

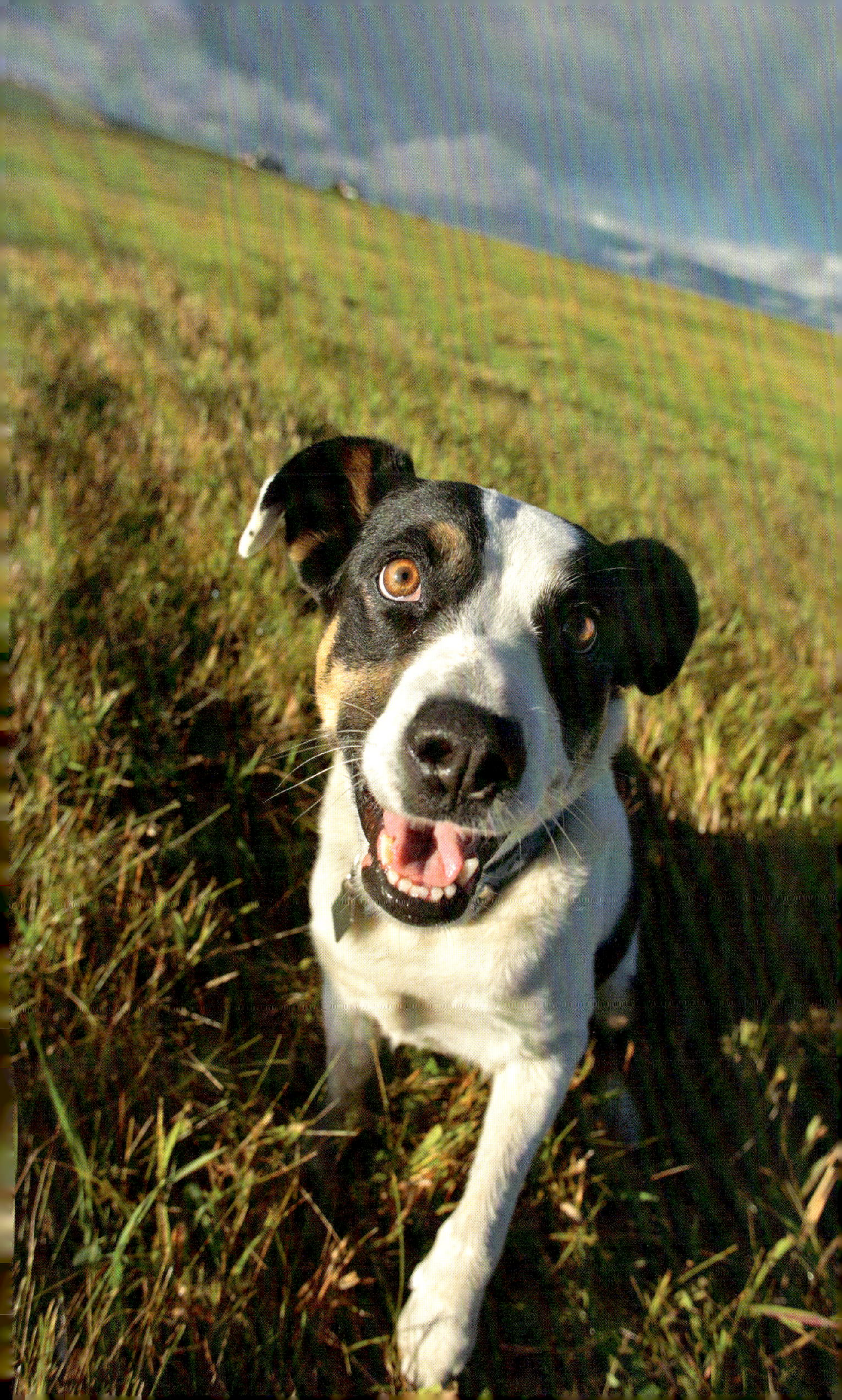

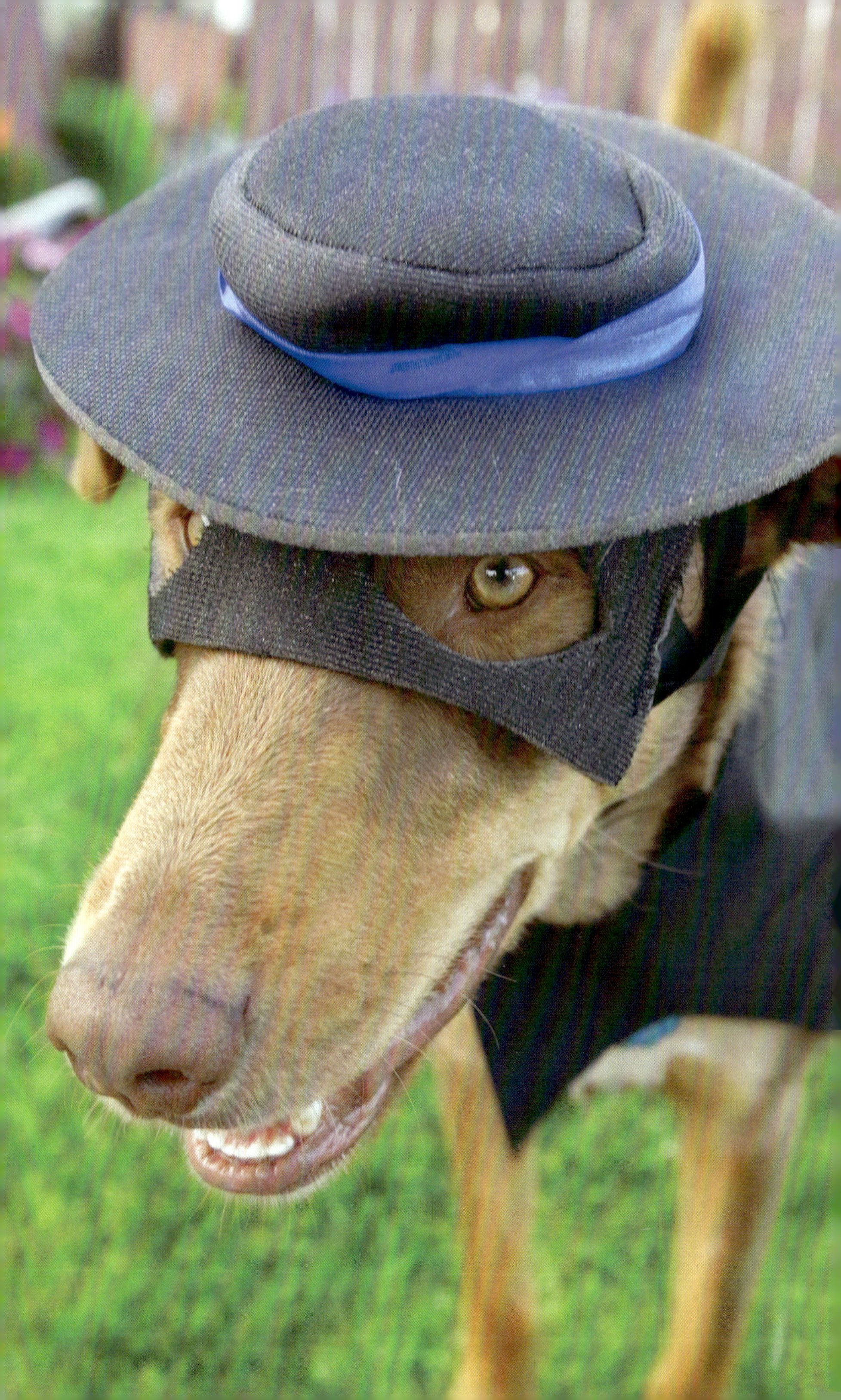

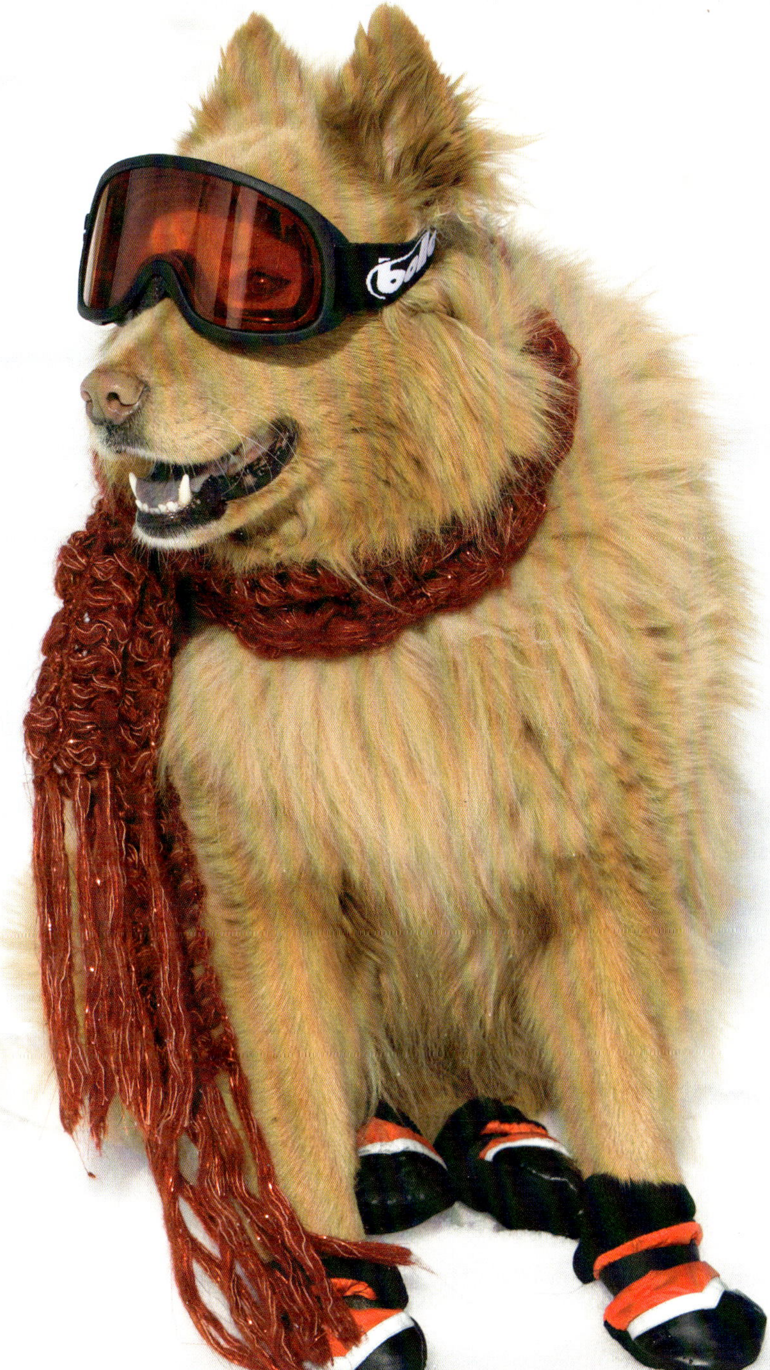

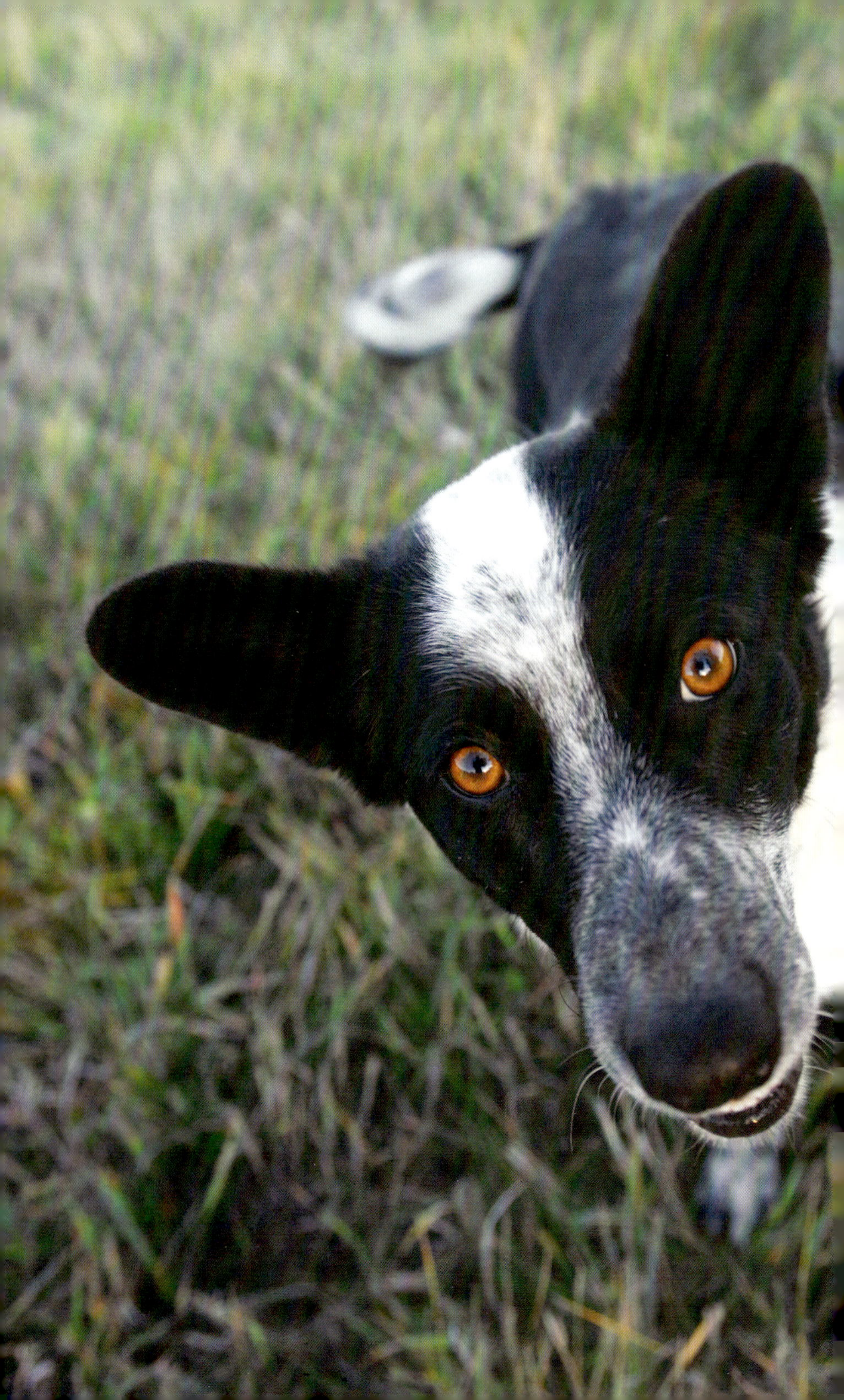

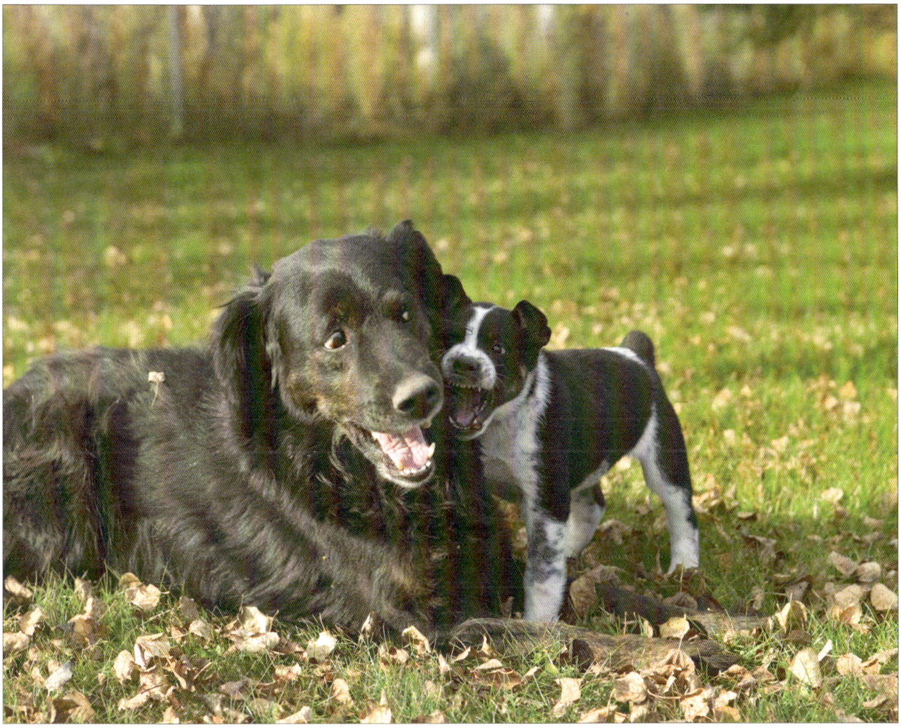

opposite:
A dog can save a human's life just as a human can save a dog's life. An "angel on four legs," Abby gave her owner the inspiration to persevere when life got tough.

above:
At first, Bubba wanted nothing to do with the new puppy. Within a week, however, Bubba and Rocky were laughing over shared jokes and playing like old friends.

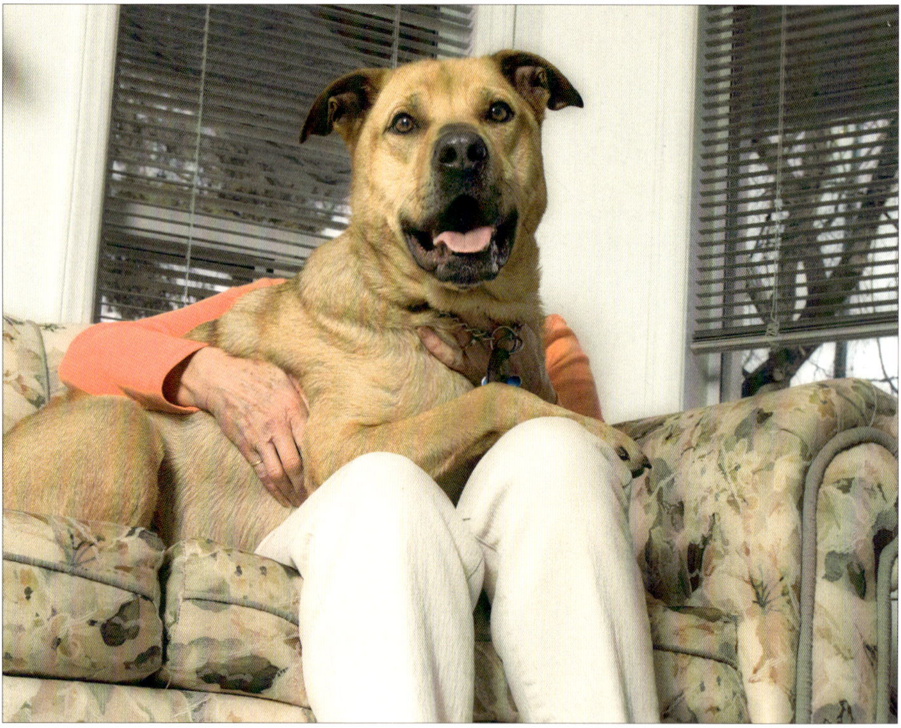

above:
Rawson loves nothing more than to squeeze himself onto his owner's lap and watch television.

opposite:
What is it about dogs and baths? You feel as though you have stripped them of their dignity when you throw them in the tub, yet they will happily traipse through mud puddles with reckless abandon. (Kiko pictured here)

page 58:
Gypsy, who looks like a border collie, has a great personality. She is a wonderful family dog.

page 59:
Small dogs often exhibit the "little dog complex:" what they lack in size they more than make up for in attitude. Perched atop this rock, Bronti surveys the land like a queen on a throne.

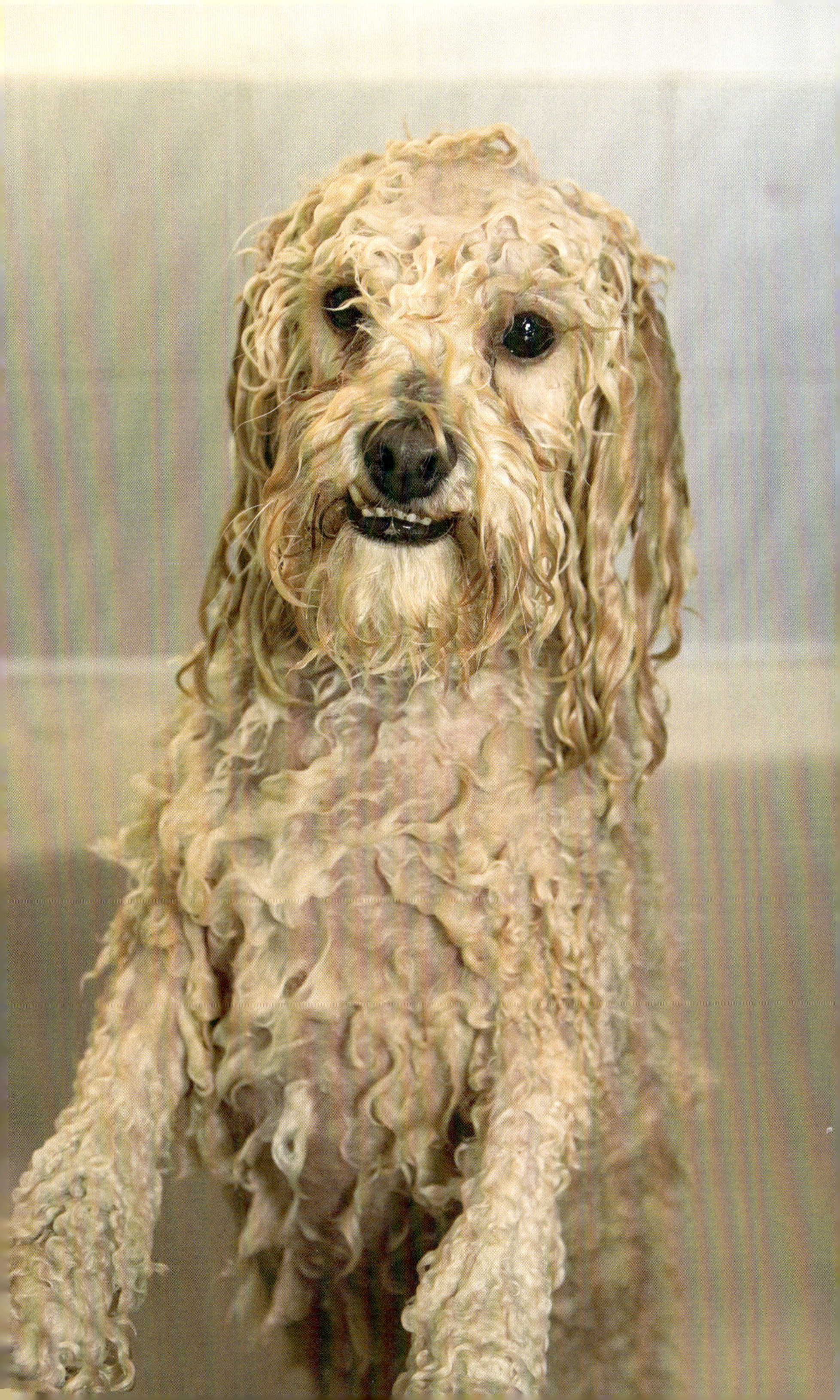

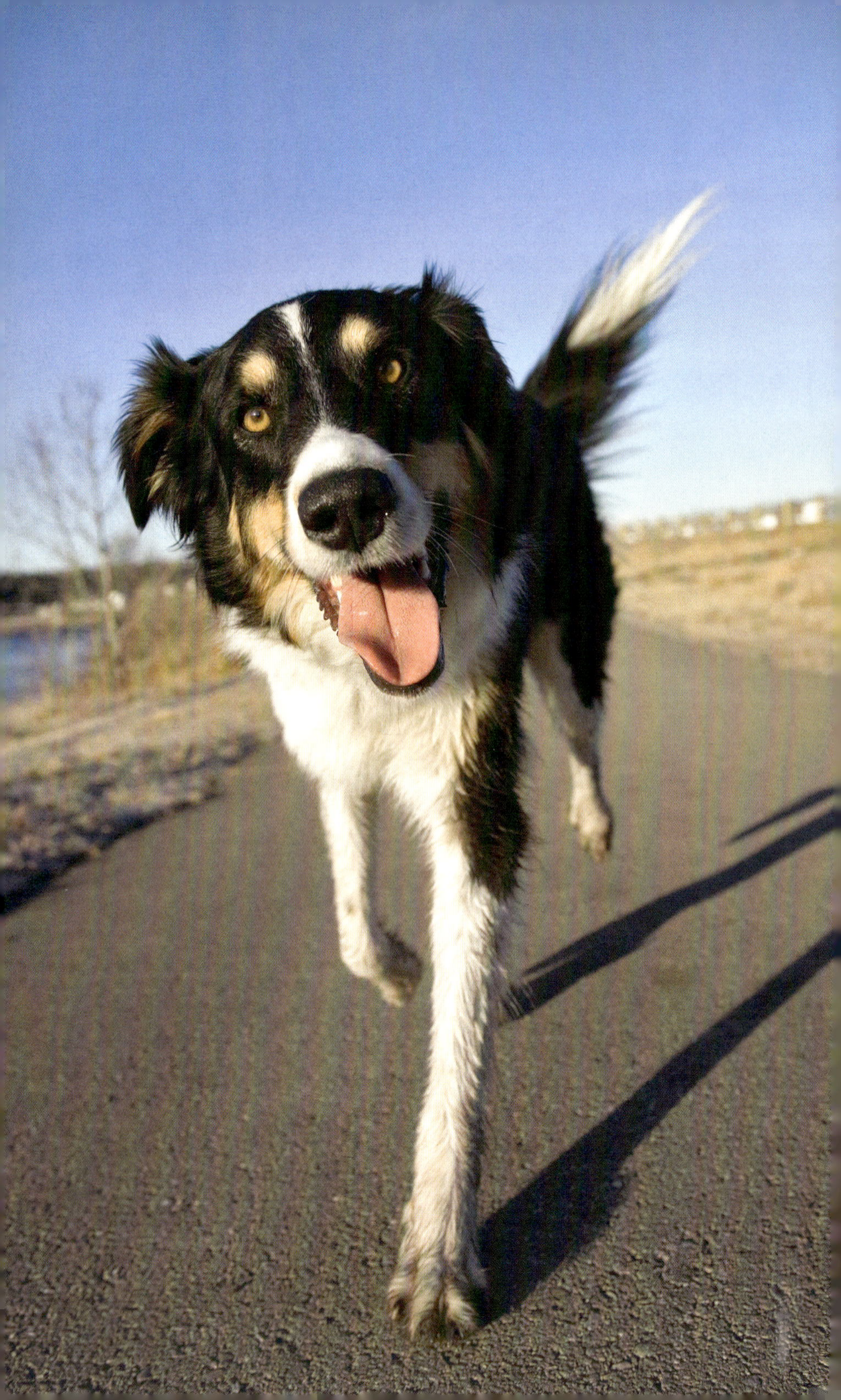

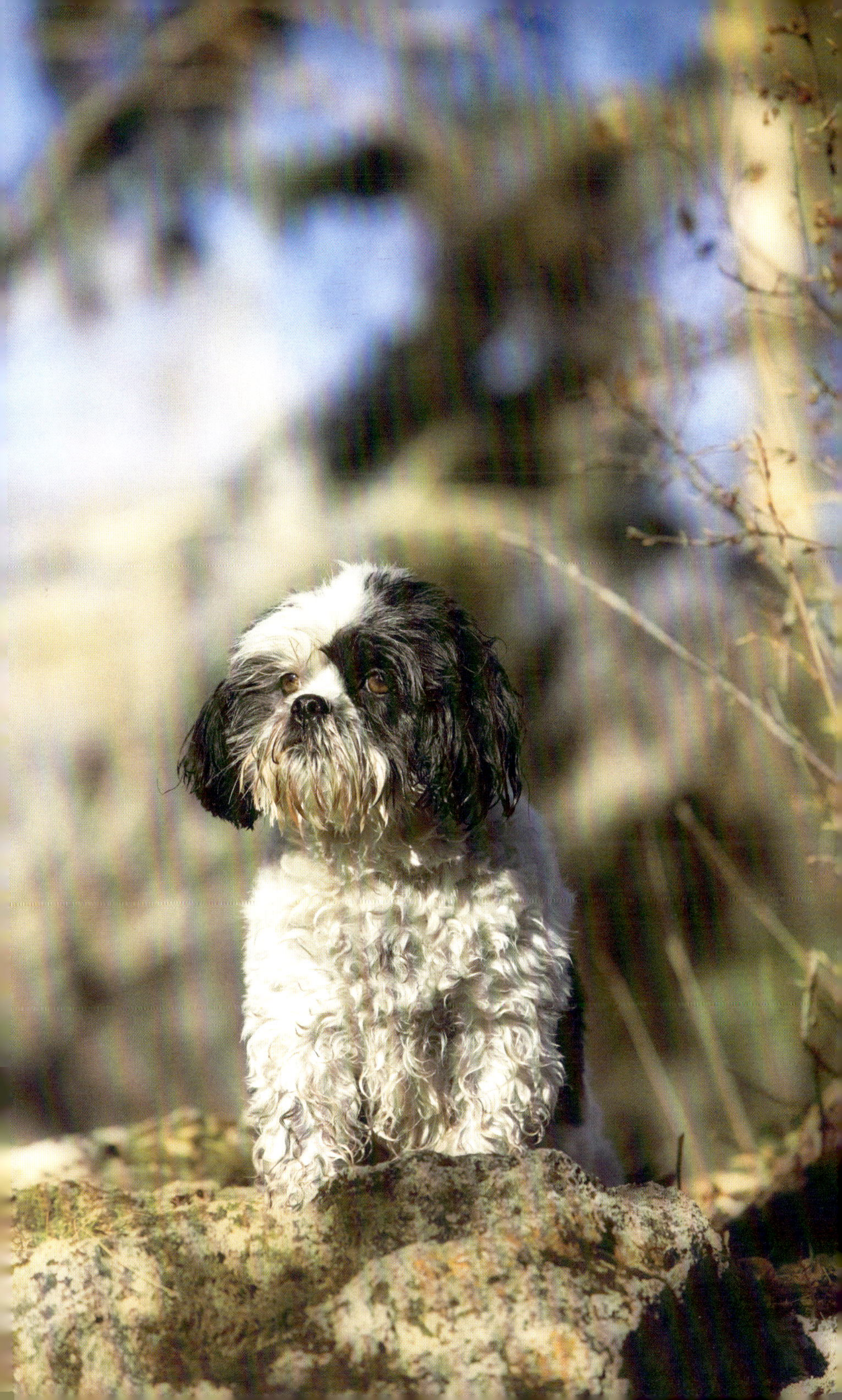

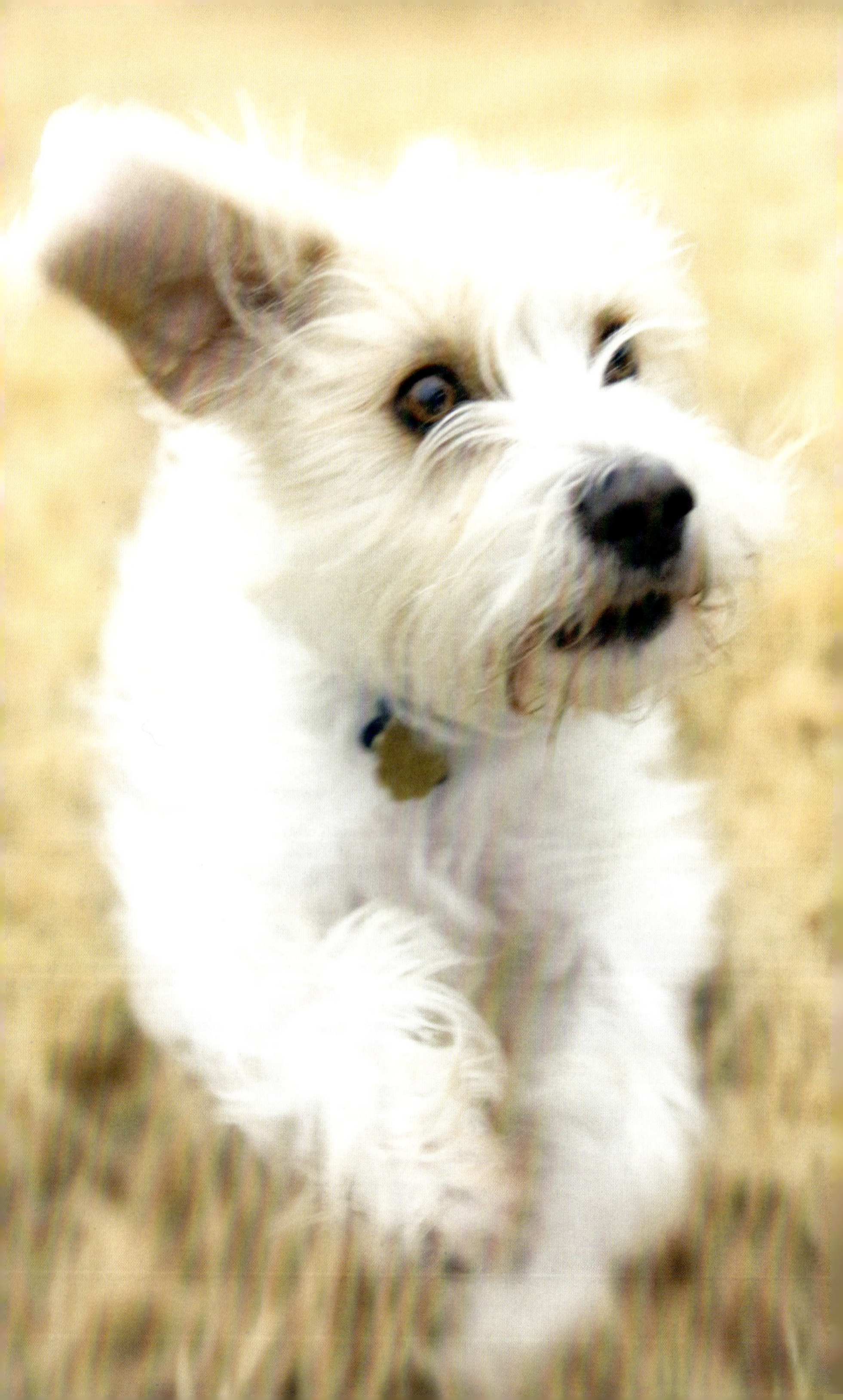

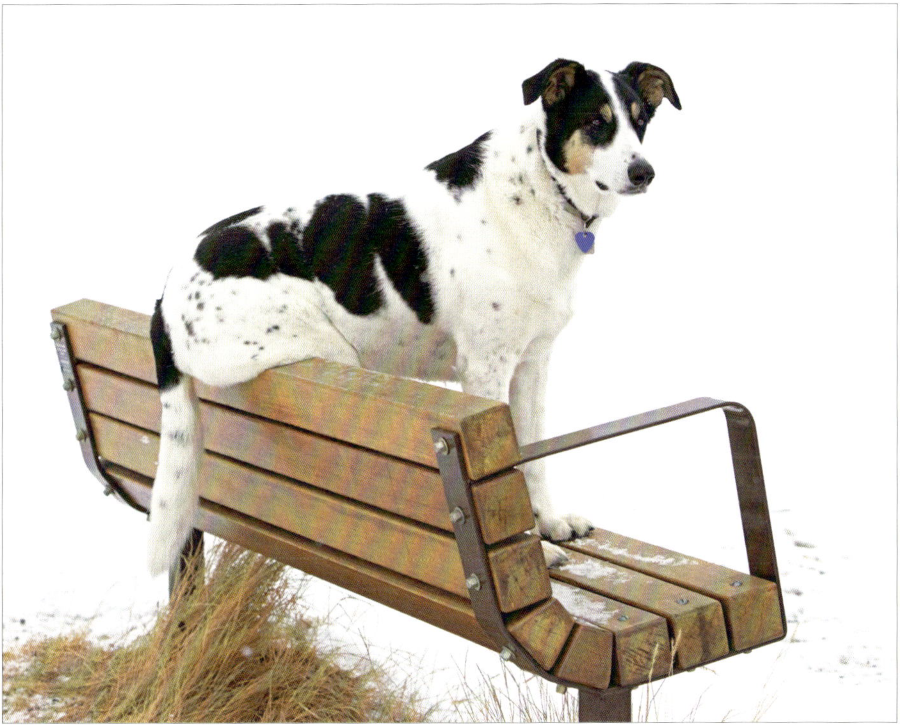

opposite:
Sammy has mastered the art of living in the moment and enjoying what the dog park has to offer.

above:
At the local dog park, everyone knows Tess as "the dog who sits on the bench."

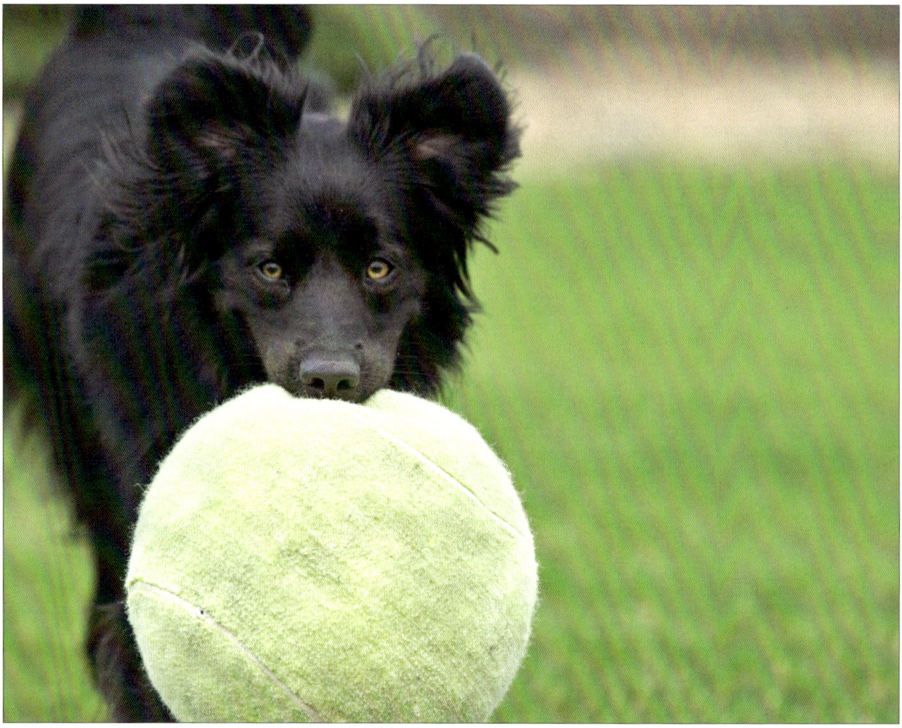

above:
No ball is too big or small for Ruby. Really!

opposite:
This terrier cross dreams of flying — perhaps the wings and goggles will help.

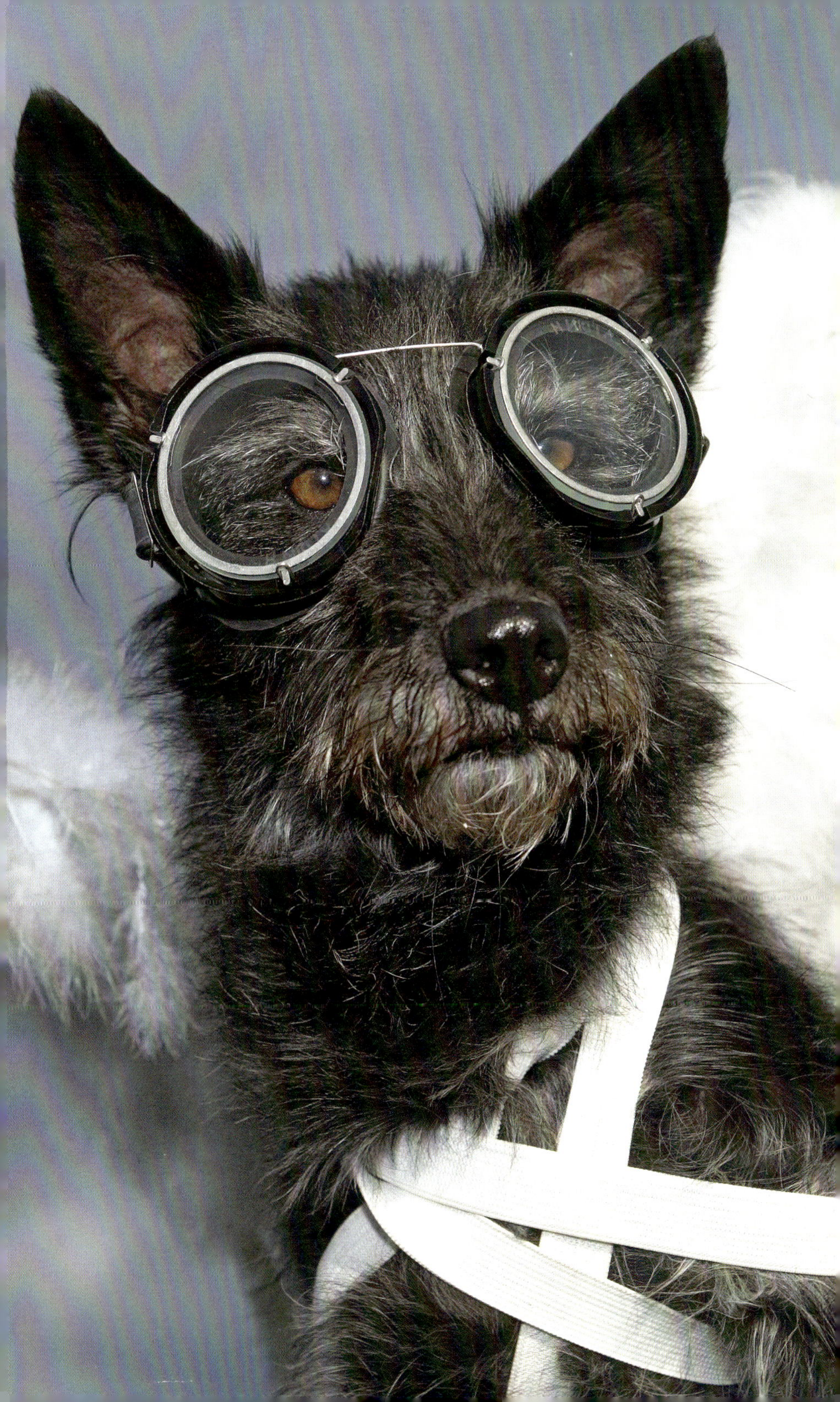

ABOUT THE PHOTOGRAPHER

Darwin Wiggett is one of Canada's top landscape photographers and has numerous books to his credit including *Dances With Light — The Canadian Rockies, How to Photograph the Canadian Rockies, Niagara Falls, Amazing Photos — Alberta Landscapes, Amazing Photos — Niagara Falls,* and *Amazing Photos — The Canadian Rockies.* This is Darwin's first foray into pet photography. Darwin lives in Water Valley, Alberta, with his happy mutt, Brando. For more information or to contact Darwin, you can visit www.darwinwiggett.com.

PHOTO CREDITS